W. Holman Bentley

Life on the Kongo

W. Holman Bentley

Life on the Kongo

ISBN/EAN: 9783743334465

Manufactured in Europe, USA, Canada, Australia, Japa

Cover: Foto ©Andreas Hilbeck / pixelio.de

Manufactured and distributed by brebook publishing software (www.brebook.com)

W. Holman Bentley

Life on the Kongo

BY
REV. W. HOLMAN BENTLEY,
BAPTIST MISSIONARY TO THE KONGO.

REVISED AND ENLARGED.

PACIFIC PRESS PUBLISHING COMPANY,
OAKLAND, CAL.,
SAN FRANCISCO, NEW YORK AND LONDON.

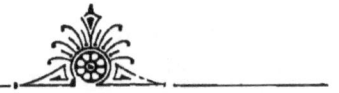

LIFE ON THE KONGO

PREFACE.

The great central African region, drained by the Kongo River and its numerous branches, is in many respects the choicest portion of the "Dark Continent." The latest to be thrown open to the inspection of the world, it is coming to the front at a pace that bids fair, in the near future, to give it the most prominent place among the newly-discovered regions of the world. It is well watered, well timbered, comprises the richest of soils, and, with the completion of a couple of railroad lines now in course of construction, will be easy of access in a commercial way.

The Kongo Free State, otherwise known as the International Free State, which includes a considerable portion of the Kongo country, affords an independent government favorable to great prosperity. This State is set apart by the united consent of the European governments which have been contending for superiority in Africa. Its independence has the pledged protection of all the governments which control adjoining territory, and their very rivalry is the best security their pledge could have. The freedom of the government and of the trade of this vast region renders it a most favorable territory for missionary work.

Most of the matter contained in this work was written about the year 1885, but it has been revised and supplemented by additional matter gleaned from reports of missionaries and other explorers of a more recent date. The information herein contained has the merit of being the product of personal observation on the part of the author and other well-known parties who have themselves traversed the ground of which they speak.

Hoping that this little volume will fill the want of a short and simple, though comprehensive, story of the new-old empire of the wonderful Kongo, the publishers confidently give it a place in the rank of books for young people. At the same time many older readers will find much of interest in these pages that they never have known before.

CONTENTS.

CHAPTER I.
Discovery of the Kongo — — — — — — 11

CHAPTER II.
Physical Features of the Kongo — — — — — 19

CHAPTER III.
Vegetation and Climate — — — — — — 30

CHAPTER IV.
The Inhabitants — — — — — — — 39

CHAPTER V.
Home Life on the Kongo — — — — — 59

CHAPTER VI.
Religious Ideas of the Natives — — — — — 74

CHAPTER VII.
Cannibalism, Freemasonry, and Charms — — — 88

CHAPTER VIII.
Missions in Central Africa — — — — — 105

CHAPTER IX.
Missions on the Kongo River — — — — — 114

CONTENTS.

CHAPTER X.

Londa Land - - - - - - - - - 136

CHAPTER XI.

Interesting Sketches - - - - - - - 149

ILLUSTRATIONS.

	PAGE.
The Kongo, near Bayneston Station - - *Frontispiece.*	
Henry M. Stanley - - - - - - -	13
A Woman and Her Load - - - - - -	25
A Scene on the River - - - - - - -	37
Ngombe Warrior - - - - - - -	41
Manner of Dressing the Hair - - - - -	60
Smoking a Pipe - - - - - - -	62
Caravan Crossing a River - - - - - -	71
A Village in the Kongo Country - - - -	99
The Mission Boat, Plymouth - - - - -	117
Transporting a Section of the Boat - - - - -	121
Putting Sections of the Boat together - - - -	129
Map Showing Location of Missions in Central Africa in 1885 - - - - - - - - -	147

Life on the Kongo.

CHAPTER I.

DISCOVERY OF THE KONGO.

IN 1484 Diogo Cam, a Portuguese navigator, first sighted the mouth of the Kongo River. Four centuries have since elapsed, and only now have we the definite knowledge of the course of that mighty flood. Seven years after the discovery of the river, an embassy was sent to San Salvador, the capital of the Kongo country. Roman Catholic missionaries followed, who in time penetrated some two hundred and fifty miles into the interior. They made, however, San Salvador their headquarters and cathedral city, but were finally expelled by the governor of Angola some one hundred and thirty years ago. They appear to have kept away from the river; what records of their work remain, throw no light as to its course. The slave trade flourished in the mouth of the river, but in the interior the land remained unknown.

In 1816 Captain Tuckey was commissioned by the British Admiralty to endeavor to solve the mystery, and was instructed to ascertain whether there was any connection between the Niger and the Kongo. This ill-fated expedition penetrated to a distance of one hundred and fifty miles from the coast. And this was the extent of our knowledge of its lower course until recently.

In 1871 Dr. Livingstone, traveling westward from the Lake Tanganyika, discovered a great river flowing northward, called by the natives Lualaba. After three and a half months he returned to the Tanganika, and finally striking south, died at Ilala, on the south of Lake Bangweolo, the upper waters of the Kongo-Lualaba, in April, 1873.

Lieutenant Cameron was commissioned by the Royal Geographical Society of Great Britain to carry fresh supplies and aid to Dr. Livingstone, but met his dead body being conveyed to the coast by his faithful servants. Continuing his journey with the material he hoped to deliver to the doctor, he crossed the Tanganyika, and reached Nyangwe, the point where Dr. Livingstone had first sighted the Lualaba. He would have followed the course of the mysterious river, but was unable to induce his men to attempt the solution of the problem, and striking southwards skirted the lower edge of the Kongo Basin, and reached the west coast at Benguela in November, 1875.

HENRY M. STANLEY.

In 1874 the London *Daily Telegraph* and New York *Herald* combined to send Mr. Stanley to Africa, to complete the geographical discoveries of Dr. Livingstone.

In *Les Belges au Congo*, the excellent Christmas number of *Le Mouvement Geographique*, the official organ of the International African Association, we have a sketch of the life of Stanley, the greatest living explorer. Born at Denbigh, in North Wales, in 1840, John Rowlands lost his father at two years of age. He was educated at the parish school of St. Asaph. At the age of sixteen he worked his passage to New Orleans, where he obtained employment in the house of a merchant named Stanley. He rose rapidly in favor and esteem, until the sudden death of his employer destroyed his hopes. Assuming the name of his benefactor, Henry Moreland Stanley was enrolled in the Confederate army when the War of Rebellion broke out in 1861. He was made prisoner at the battle of Pittsburg Landing, in 1862, but effected his escape. Constantly exposed to arrest as an escaped prisoner, he engaged himself as a sailor in the Federal marine, in which he obtained rapid promotion, becoming secretary to the captain of the Ticonderoga, and later held the same position under the admiral.

He accompanied his vessel on a European cruise, and obtained his discharge at the end of the war. He was next correspondent of the Missouri *Democrat* and the New York *Tribune*, and later became traveling correspondent to the New York *Herald*, for which he accompanied the British forces during the Abyssinian and Ashantee wars. When those wars were over, he made a journey through Asia Minor, the Caucasus, and Persia to India, thence by Egypt to Spain, where he received his commission to find Livingstone.

That successful expedition marked him as the man to carry on further exploratory work in Africa; and when the news of Dr. Livingstone's death reached Europe, fired with the desire to carry on the work of the great doctor, he gladly accepted the commission of the *Daily Telegraph* and New York *Herald*.

Starting from Zanzibar November 17, 1874, he circumnavigated the Lakes Victoria-Nyanza and Tanganyika for the first time, carefully charting them. Thence he struck across to Nyangwe. In spite of all the obstacles and difficulties that had hindered others, his great determination, his resources, and knowledge of the Swahili language, enabled him to induce his men to follow him down the river.

He recalled to their minds the long, weary marches, and the terrible dark forests of Urega through which they had passed, and told how much easier it would be to sit in canoes, and paddle down this great river, which must flow into the sea. They agreed, and met the first serious impediment to navigation at the equator, where a series of seven cataracts in forty miles caused them to transport their canoes overland round these obstacles.

Clear of these Stanley Falls, they had an uninterrupted course for one thousand and sixty miles, the river widening out in some places to as much as twenty-five miles in breadth, studded with low, sandy, tree-covered islands. As he neared the end of this grand reach of waterway, hills appeared, the river narrowed, and the banks grew steeper until they towered a thousand feet above him. The river widened out once more into a pool some seventy miles in circumference, which is now named Stanley Pool, at the western end of which the explorer heard the thunder of the Ntamu Cataracts.

From this point his difficulties were to be of a different nature. Along the one thousand miles of clear waterway which he had just passed, he had been exposed to the constant attacks of wild, fierce savages, now he had to struggle with a wilder, fiercer river. The next one hundred miles occupied four months. Dragging his canoes overland, past the Ntamu Cataracts, he took once more to the water, only to find another cataract a few miles lower down.

This was his constant experience, while the porterage past these obstacles often involved the conveyance of his heavy canoes, stores, provisions, etc., seven hundred and one thousand feet up the steep banks of the river, four or five miles overland, and down again into the deep gorge. Stores were running short, food was scarce, canoes were lost in the rapids, some of his men were drowned, including

Frank Pocock, his only surviving white companion. Privations, sickness, and murderous natives had thinned his ranks, but he struggled on.

Clearing the Ntombo Mataka Falls, he found a reach of ninety miles of very bad, but navigable, water, and at the end of which were the great Isangila Falls. There, learning that he was within a few days' journey of factories and white men, he left the river, and his weary company toiled over the steep quartz hills, and reached Mboma in August, 1877, in an almost starving condition.

A year of drought and great scarcity of food had added much to his difficulties. However, the journey was accomplished, the Kongo River had been traced, the highway into the heart of Africa had been explored. Taking his people down the last quiet sixty miles of the river, he arranged for their return to Zanzibar, *via* the Cape of Good Hope. Having seen them safe home again, and rewarded their devotion and toil, he reached England to announce his great discovery.

CHAPTER II.

PHYSICAL FEATURES OF THE KONGO.

ROUGHLY, we may describe the basin of the Kongo as extending from the fifth degree of north latitude to the twelfth degree of south latitude, and from the hills skirting the coast of the Atlantic Ocean to the thirty-first degree of east longitude, having an area of one million fifty-six thousand and two hundred square miles.

Along what is known as the southwest coast of Africa, from the Gulf of Biafra southwards, stretches a ridge of hill country. It commences about fifty to seventy miles inland, and is about three hundred miles in width. In some parts it attains an elevation of five thousand or more feet, but the general altitude near the Kongo is from two thousand to two thousand five hundred feet above the level of the sea. It is really a belt or elevated plateau; rich soil is to be found on the summits of the hills, but the whole has been torn and worn by the rains; little streams have in time cut out deep gorges, the sides of which are being further eroded, or eaten out, until what was once a rolling table-land appears as a chaos of hills; only from a few heights can one gain a fair idea of the nature of the country.

This plateau belt forms the western watershed of the Kongo River, and on its seaward slopes gives rise to many unimportant streams, of which the Cameroons, Gaboon, Ogowai, Kwilu, Chiloango, Mbidiji (Ambrize), Loje, and Kwanza are the principal. The Ogowai is the most important, and has been employed by M. de Brazza for the French Government, which has now annexed its entire basin. It is navigable for some one hundred and fifty miles for vessels of light draught; but beyond this its course is much impeded by cataracts.

This water-torn plateau country, with its little useless rivers, has presented a formidable obstacle to exploration, and has served to throw all interior water into the Kongo. To the north of the Great Basin stretches the highlands of the unknown countries, which form also the watershed of the Shari and the Nile. Eastward stretches the hill country to the western slope of Lakes Victoria and Albert-Nyanza, including in its border Lake Tanganyika, while to the south is the watershed of the Zambezi.

This great circle of hills probably inclosed at one time an immense fresh-water lake, of an area of a million and a half square miles, which at length, overflowing at its weakest point, formed the outlet which we to-day call the Kongo River. The immense flood thus released, tore out the deep gorge, which is now one thousand to one thousand five hundred feet below the main level. There are signs in some parts of changes in its course, one notably in the Bundi Valley, thirty-five miles from Vivi, which was at one time, undoubtedly, a channel of the Kongo; there are other valleys also presenting that appearance, the levels, entrances, and exits of which would lead one to conclude that such had been the case.

If a cross section of the Kongo Valley were taken about the middle of the cataract region, there would be first an ascent from the river of from three hundred to five hundred feet in about one-third of a mile, then a much steadier rise of some five hundred to seven hundred feet in two miles, and then a rise of another five hundred to seven hundred feet in eight miles, with a further steady rise for five miles, so that the actual valley in the cataract region might be estimated roughly at from twenty to thirty miles in breadth. The river itself varies from three hundred yards to one and a half or two miles wide at mid-flood, while the difference between the highest water of the rainy season and the lowest in the dry season varies from forty feet in the most rainy parts to about three feet on the lower river.

To the geologist the country between the coast and Stanley Pool is best studied along the river. The first low hills approach near to the mouth of the river, which is about seven miles wide, and, unlike the Nile, has no delta; the next step in the plateau occurs at five miles west of Mboma, fifty miles from the coast, where the tops of the hills are from five hundred to seven hundred feet in height. There we find a red clay, yielding copal, above granitic rocks. The banks grow steeper, and the river narrows, until at Vivi the first serious obstacle is met, the plateau level being about one thousand seven hundred feet, and the river about six hundred yards wide. Just above this is the fierce Yelala Cataract; indeed, nowhere can you properly speak of falls; a drop of fifty feet, which would be a fine scene on an ordinary river, is almost disregarded by the Kongo. The bed of a cataract must be of very hard rock, and down this inclined plane, the river, pressed tightly by the hills, rushes with fearful velocity, leaping in mad waves, foaming and raging at its rocky obstacles. In some of the milder cataracts it rushes down a swirling mound of water, which, projected into the quieter low level at the foot of the cataract, races on as a heap of waters for nearly half a mile, before it consents to swirl about to the level of the waters around it. Fierce up-currents run along the shore at such points, which would draw boats or canoes into the swirling current, while along the edges of these counter-currents are great whirlpools, giving way to each other, disappearing, and breaking up into "caldrons," the whole surface heaving and seething in mad tumult. In a creek three miles below the Ntombo Cataract we have watched the heaving waters. The water would flow outwards from the creek, then, meeting the impulse of a fresh wave, would flow back until it would remain stationary for some twenty seconds, often two feet higher than what it was a moment before. This backward and forward flow of the creek occurs about every two minutes.

At Vivi the country is much eroded; granitic rocks, schist, mica, gneiss, and quartz are exposed. The hillsides are rock strewn, and the country is wild and desolate, covered with weak grass and stunted, gnarled trees. In the more level spots rich soil has collected, and the natives cultivate there their cassava, ground-nuts, and other productions. This is the nature of the country for the next fifty miles. Near the river is a chaos of hills; further away is a rolling plateau, covered with strong grass and stunted trees. The tops of these *nzanza*, by Mr. Stanley's careful survey, vary but fifty feet over stretches of forty miles. Above Isangila limestone crops up with slaty rocks; the main level near the river is lower, and traversed by straight ridges of hills running parallel with the coast, and from five to ten miles apart. Clear of the limestone, the country is once more a torn plateau; slate and shale abound, until at two hundred miles from the coast occurs a very marked step of seven hundred feet. Here the country is from two thousand three hundred to two thousand five hundred feet above the sea, and so continues, the rock being a red or purple sandstone. Several higher ridges cross the country as you near Stanley Pool, and are cut abruptly by the gorge of the river. Stanley Pool is a widening out of the river in a weak point among the hills. This marks the head of the cataract region, the water level being about one thousand feet above the sea. The plateau country continues for one hundred and fifty miles further, when hills disappear, and the main level appears to be about one thousand one hundred feet above the sea. From Irebu, two hundred and fifty miles above the Pool, to Stanley Falls the banks are forest-clad. The country then divides itself into three regions between the coast and Stanley Falls: the lower river, one hundred miles; cataract region, two hundred miles (nearly three hundred miles in winding course); the upper river, one thousand and sixty miles; or, coast level, fifty miles; plateau level, four hundred miles; central level, nine hundred miles, of which eight hundred miles are forest-clad banks.

The cataract region is the obstacle that has kept so long secret this great highway; but that passed, on the upper river there are one thousand one hundred miles of unimpeded navigation, while the main branches of the river are estimated at two thousand miles; beyond the Stanley Falls stretch another two thousand miles of riverway. Two of the branches have been explored, and on each was found a lake, while the natives speak of lakes on other affluents. It is highly probable that further explorations will reveal other lake regions, all avail-

A WOMAN AND HER LOAD.

able to the steamers and boats on the upper river.

Communications in the interior are certain; but between the coast and Stanley Pool everything must be transported on native heads, until there shall be a railway. The roads from town to town are mere footpaths over the hills, while the tall, thick grass is so strong that it must be dug up and the bushes cleared before any wheeled carriage could be used. Then, again, the country is so torn, and streams in their deep gorges so abundant, that traveling is very largely a series of ascents and descents, attended by great danger.

Rev. David Charters, in speaking of the extent of the Kongo Valley, in his address before the Centenary Conference on the Protestant Missions of the World, in 1888, said:—

"The river Kongo is now recognized by many to be the highway into the Soudan and the interior of Central Africa. On arrival at Banana, on the west coast of Africa, at the mouth of the river Kongo, we changed steamers and took passage to Underhill Station, about a hundred miles up. Not far from Underhill we came to the first cataract; and from this point right on to Stanley Pool, a distance of about two hundred and twenty miles, the river is more or less impeded by cataracts. I may here say that a party of engineers are busy surveying the cataract region; they are prospecting for a railway to connect the Lower with the Upper Kongo. Following the Kongo from Stanley Pool, we have a clear and uninterrupted course of over one thousand miles of waterway, varying in width from sixteen hundred yards to sixteen miles, and extending to Stanley Falls. Following the affluents on the left bank, we are able to reach as far south as five degrees of south latitude. Ascending the Mobangi on the right bank of the river, we are able almost to reach five degrees of north latitude. As we think of the wonderful extent of country drained by this great river, we also think of the thousands who have been so long in darkness and in the shadow of death. To attempt to tell their numbers or position would simply mean failure."

Rev. George Cameron, of Stanley Pool, gives the following short description of a scene on the Kongo:—

"Looking down the river from the corner of Underhill Gardens, a fine view is had of three or four miles of its course. Though it is here seven miles below Yellala Falls—the last of the Livingstone Falls—the water is still rushing along very swiftly, perhaps making as many as ten or twelve miles an hour, when in full flood. Looked at from the hill, it has a suspiciously smooth, glassy appearance, but when one is closer it is seen to be eddying and foaming in numberless whirlpools, many of them large enough to endanger canoes or small boats venturing within their reach. It is at this point scarcely a mile broad, but what it lacks in breadth is made up in depth, it being so deep as to be practically unfathomable.

"The hills vary from about one hundred and fifty feet above the water level to three or four times that height; the hill on which the station is built is one hundred and seventy feet above the river, while just opposite is a fine bluff rising up from the water to a height of about six hundred feet. When it is added that these hills are rocky and sterile, and that there are many more such hills between the lower river and Stanley Pool, it will be readily understood that the finding of a proper route for the proposed railroad was a matter of no small difficulty.

"The Yellala Cataracts are the first of a series of some thirty-two which render navigation between Underhill and Stanley Pool an utter impossibility. When the river is high, the water rushes with terrific fury through the narrow gorges, and the scene is wild in the extreme. Nothing but being there one's self, hearing the roar and seeing the rush of the waters, can give any true idea of its grandeur."

CHAPTER III.
VEGETATION AND CLIMATE.

THE vegetation is very varied in the rock-strewn sides of the ravines; in the granitic and quartzose regions it is very bare and weak; but where the plateau level has been less disturbed, the thick maxinde (pronounced *mashinde*) grass shows the richness of the soil, while the carefully-tended farms near the towns, beautiful with the rich green of the ground-nut, thickly tangled with sweet potatoes, or jungled with cassava bushes, show what can be done with the soil by clearing and a little scratching with the hoe.

In the broader valleys, where the streams are smaller, or have done less destruction to the country, grows the giant diàdia grass, the stems often attaining two and a half inches in circumference and an average height of fifteen feet; there may be found some of the richest soil in the world. Where the diàdia has been, exists the wildest luxuriance of vegetation; palms, plantain, Indian corn, ground-nuts, yams, and all garden produce are at their best, and ever at the mercy of the elephants, who rejoice in such choice selection. In the Majinga country the native houses have to be scattered through their rich farms, and morning and night the people shout, scream, and beat their drums to frighten off these giant marauders.

It is not a forest country. Strange clumps of trees grow on the tops of the hills which mark the ancient plateau level, but the rich soil beside the streams and in the snug valleys is generally well wooded. The vegetation presents an altogether tropical appearance; the bracken, or fern, in the glades is the only thing homelike. Rich creepers drape the trees, beautiful palms lend their rare grace, and in their seasons an endless succession of beautiful flowers, from huge arums to a tiny crucifer of the richest scarlet, bright creepers, pure white stephanotis-like blossoms, rich lilies, and many other gorgeous plants and bright berries, not in such wild, packed profusion that the eye is bewildered with a blaze of beauty, but here and there with sufficient interval to permit the due appreciation of their several lovelinesses. The beauty of the leaf forms is alone a pleasure, while the tints, from the darkest green to soft yellow, delicate pink, bronze, chocolate, and bright crimson, are mysteries of color. On the rocky stream banks and on the palm stems are graceful ferns, while the *lycopodium* climbs the bushes, mingled with the beautiful *selaginella*. The scenery of the country is described in an unequaled manner by Mr. H. H. Johnston in his book, "The River Kongo." Himself an accomplished artist, he describes as only an artist can.

The vegetation suffers from the annual grass fires which sweep the country. As soon as the dry season has well begun in June, the burning commences; in some parts it does not become general until August. The grass is fired sometimes on a small scale by the children, that they may hunt their rats, but the great fires occur when the natives of a district combine for a grand hunt. For days the fire steadily sweeps along, the game flee before it, hawks wheel above the line of fire, catching the grasshoppers that seek to avoid the flames, while smaller birds catch the lesser insects. The internodes of the burning grass explode with a report like that of a pistol, and can be heard distinctly a mile distant. Women and children follow on the line to dig out the rats; and in the holes may be found rats, mice, snakes, and lizards, seeking common protection from a common danger. At night the horizon is lit up by the zigzag lines of fire, and in the daytime are seen the thick columns of smoke slowly advancing, and filling the air with a dull haze, which limits the horizon to ten or fifteen miles.

The climate of the Kongo has been unduly vilified. In common with all intertropical regions, there is a malarial fever, which has claimed many victims. It generally assumes an intermittent type, commencing with an ague "shake;" sometimes it is remittent, and combines with grave symptoms. Although the precise nature of the malarial germ is still unknown, continued study has enabled medical men to grapple much more successfully with this great enemy. So long as it was the custom to treat the fever with bleeding and calomel, it was no wonder that Africa was "the white man's grave;" that was not so much the fault of Africa as the white man's ignorance.

Traders on the coast have generally fair health, and many live to old age. Women in the mission stations and elsewhere live long on the coast. Indeed, Dr. Laws, of Livingstonia, has expressed an opinion that women, as a rule, stand the climate better than the men.

In these matters we are far readier to count up the misfortunes than to note the large proportion of those who live long and do good work in Africa.

New missions and scientific expeditions have paid the penalty for ignorance and the difficulties of pioneering; but where the experience of others can aid, and due precautions are observed, there is no reason why the Kongo should be considered more unhealthy than India generally. It is certainly possible to live on the Kongo. The writer, who was one of the first party of the Baptist Missionary Society's Kongo Mission, and has had five years' pioneering work, had not a single fever during the last two and a half years. This is rather exceptional, but speaks well as to the possibilities. Indeed, there are many reasons why the climate of India should be considered worse. The Indian temperature is far higher, dysentery and cholera are annual scourges, and liver complaints far more common.

The excellent *Observations Météorologiques* of Dr. A. von Danckelman, of the International Association (Asher & Co., Berlin), gives most interesting statistics of the Lower Kongo. The highest temperature registered by him at an elevation of three hundred and seventy-five feet was ninety-six and five-tenths degrees Fahrenheit, and the lowest fifty-three degrees, the highest mean temperature being eighty-three degrees. The general midday temperature in the house in the hot season is eighty degrees to eighty-five degrees, and at night seventy-five degrees to eighty degrees. On the coast a cool breeze blows in from the sea from about eleven o'clock in the morning, commencing somewhat later in proportion to the distance in the interior. This same cool sea breeze blows freshly on the upper river, and even when high temperatures can be taken in the sun, the air is cool. Very frequently thick clouds cover the sky and temper the heat. In this respect the Kongo compares very favorably with India, and with other parts of the African coast. On the Kongo a *punkah*, or fan, is quite unnecessary at any time, in a house built on a reasonable site.

The rainy season commences in the cataract region about September 15, the greatest amount of rain falling in November and April, with the "little rains" about Christmastime. The wet season closes about May 15. The rise of the river from the northern rains commences about August, reaching its height about January 1, when it falls rapidly until April 1. It then rises rapidly a second time but not so high as before, about May 1; it then steadily falls until August. These dates may vary a fortnight, or even three weeks; that is to say, they may occur so much earlier, but seldom later.

The rain generally falls at night, often with a violent tornado soon after sundown. Heavy clouds appear on the horizon, the tornado arch advances, the wind lulls, and with breathless suspense everything prepares for the onslaught of the storm. A dull roar strikes the ear. The hiss of rain, with fierce gusts of wind, is heard, and in a moment the deluge is upon you. Wild wind, torrents of rain, incessant peals of thunder, flashes of lightning, are almost continuous. The whole world seems to be in turmoil. After an hour or two the fury of the storm is spent, and heavy rain continues for a while.

Considering the intensity of the electric disturbance, accidents by lightning are rare. One or two cases only have been noted thus far: The mission boat on the Cameroons River was struck, and three people on board killed; a house of the International Association was fired; the same thing occurred in a native village. Occasionally a tree is struck.

Game is not by any means abundant. Several species of antelope are found, the most common being the harnessed antelope (*Tragelaphus scriptus*). Elephants are numerous in some parts, but are very seldom hunted. Leopards are found throughout the country. There are two species of buffaloes on the upper river; west of Stanley Pool they are less numerous, and are found in fewer places. The gorilla is reported some sixty miles north of Stanley Pool. The chimpanzee has been heard of, but not seen. Many monkeys inhabit the woods. The jackal is not uncommon; but the lion, which was common until fifty years ago, has disappeared over the district between the Kwangu and the mouth of the river. Hippopotami are very numerous; three varieties of crocodile infest the rivers. Fish in great variety are caught by the natives in traps and nets and by hooks and spearing. Whitebait fishing affords occupation to many men in the cataract regions. By day they sit on the rocks waiting for the gleam of a shoal of fish; and when one appears, in an instant they have divested themselves of their scanty clothes, and rush into the strong, shallow water with their nets—not unlike a shrimper's net—each one a little beyond the other, and often are well rewarded for their trouble. Their take is then dried in the sun and sold in the market.

There is an endless variety of bird life, which, as the mating season nears, dons brighter and more striking-colored plumage. One of the most numerous kinds is the grey parrot, great flocks of which fly home in the evenings, whistling and screaming, the happiest birds there are.

A SCENE ON THE RIVER.

CHAPTER IV.

THE INHABITANTS.

THE inhabitants of Africa have been divided into six great races. Their languages form the basis of such division. Mr. R. N. Cust, the secretary of the Royal Asiatic Society, has recently published a valuable work on the languages of Africa, and the colored map accompanying it presents the distribution of races very graphically to the eye. To the north we find the Semitic race; in the Sahara, on the Nile, in Abyssinia, and in Somali land, a Hamitic race, speaking languages allied to Ethiopic; from Gambia to the mouths of the Niger, the negro race, of whom the Ashantees are types.

Interspersed among the negro and Hamitic races are detached peoples, speaking languages of the Nuba Fullah group, of whom the Massai, among whom Mr. Thomson has been traveling, to the east of the Victoria-Nyanza, may be taken as typical of the rest.

To the south of all these is the great Bantu (men) race. A line drawn eastward from the Gulf of Biafra to the Indian Ocean will mark roughly the boundary of this greatest of the African races. Near to the Cape of Good Hope are found the Hottentot Bushman, a degraded race, who appear to have been the aborigines, but now, driven to the remotest corner, are still yielding to the stronger Bantus.

Not very promising was the aspect which the wild people dwelling on the banks of the Kongo River presented to Mr. Stanley during his first journey through these unknown regions. As he approached a village, the great war drums and horns thundered through the woods, canoes were manned, and, apparently without the remotest reason, they proceeded to attack the white man with his little flock.

Fierce, wild savagery, loathsome cannibalism and cruelty, the densest darkness and degradation of heathenism—such was the aspect as the two white men, with some one hundred and fifty followers, endeavored quietly and peaceably to paddle in midstream past the villages.

We have talked with these people about this humiliating phase of humanity.

"Why did you attack the *mundele* [white man]?"

"We did not, but we were going to."

"Why? Sit down, and tell us all about it."

This we said to a Zombo slave of the Bayansi of Bolobo, who had been sold by his countrymen for ivory, when scarcely more than a baby. His forehead scored with the tribal mark of his master, he

NGOMBE WARRIOR.

was in bearing and speech a thorough Mubangi, but remembered his old language, as there are many such slaves on the upper river.

"The news reached us," he said, "that a white man and his followers were coming down the river. Everyone above us had attacked him for the honor and glory of having fought one of the mysterious whites we hear of, and for whose cloth we trade. We could not let the opportunity pass; had we done so, we should have been behind the rest, and become the ridicule of the river. When we went to trade, and joined the dance in friendly towns, the girls would sing how their braves had fought the white man, while the Bolobo people had hidden in the grass like women. We manned our canoes, and hid behind the long point above our town; but a little above us the white man crossed to the other side of the river. We waited to see what would happen, and soon one of our people came from the opposite towns, and told us that the white man was buying food, and giving beads, brass wire, and glorious things. We quickly filled our canoes with plantain, cassava pudding, fowls, etc., and hurried over, and so we did not fight after all."

That was the beginning of better days for Mr. Stanley. The story as we heard it at Stanley Pool explains in a measure the persistent savage attacks.

It was long surmised that some dwarf races, said to be scattered through the Bantu countries, were of this aboriginal stock, but for some time no satisfactory opportunities were offered for ascertaining the truth. The doubt of the existence of actual tribes of dwarfs has, however, been dispelled by Mr. Stanley's latest expedition. He reports having passed through villages of dwarfs, and describes individual specimens. He describes a queen who was brought in to see him, as being four feet four inches in height and about twenty years old. She was of a light brown complexion, with broad, round face, large eyes, and small but full lips. She was adorned with three polished iron rings around the neck, the ends of which were coiled like a watch spring, and three iron rings in each ear. She had a quiet, modest appearance, although but partially covered with clothing, which was of bark cloth.

Another young woman is described as being about seventeen years of age and thirty-three inches high. She was a perfectly-formed little colored lady, with not a little gracefulness and a very interesting face. Her color was about that of a Southern States quadroon, or nearly that of yellow ivory. "Her eyes were magnificent, but absurdly large for such a small creature, almost as large as those of a young gazelle."

Near one of these dwarf villages, Mr. Stanley's men captured some of the little people and brought them into camp. In his book, "In Darkest Africa" (Scribner's Sons, New York), the great explorer tells of the incident as follows:—

"We had four women and a boy, and in them I

saw two distinct types. One evidently belonged to that same race described as the Akka, with small, cunning, monkey eyes, close, and deeply set. The four others possessed large, round eyes, broad, round foreheads, round faces, small hands and feet, lower jaws projecting forward slightly, figures well formed though small, and of a bricky complexion. . . . The monkey-eyed woman had a very mischievous look, large lips overhanging her chin, prominent abdomen, narrow, flat chest, sloping shoulders, long arms, very short lower limbs, and feet turned greatly inwards. This was an extremely low, degraded, almost a bestial type of humanity.

"One of the others was a mother, though she could not have seen her seventeenth year. Her complexion was bright and healthy; her eyes were brilliant, round, and large; her upper lip had the peculiar cut of the Wambutti—the upper edge curving upward with a sharp angle, with a curl up of the skin as though it had contracted. . . The color of the lips was pinkish. The hands were small, fingers long and delicate, but skinny and puckered; the feet measured seven inches, and her height was four feet four inches. So perfect were the proportions of this girl-mother that she appeared at first to be but an undersized woman, her low stature being the result of some accidental circumstances. But when we placed some of our Zanzibar boys of fifteen or sixteen years old by her side, and finally placed a woman of the agricultural natives near her, it was clear to everyone that these small creatures were a distinct race."

One of these dwarfs, a woman, was brought to England by some African travelers, and on being taken to Dublin was described in a news item as being "thirty-six inches in height, of well-developed body and jet black complexion. She had a peculiarly monkeyish expression, and a nose so flat that the lower part of the face resembled closely the muzzle of an animal. She has learned some English, and is free to talk. One of the first accomplishments her civilized captors have taught her is to smoke cigarettes."

Of the Bantus the Zulu Kaffirs may be the best-known types, although they have borrowed from the Hottentots the clicks that so much disfigure their language. With the exception of the dwarfs, the inhabitants of the Kongo basin are all Bantus. Mr. Stanley estimates that there are a thousand tribes in this basin, most if not all of which have had a common origin many generations in the past.

As before stated, language is the basis of such classification. With the other races they have nothing in common. In roots, grammatical construction and all distinguishing features of language, the Bantu dialects have a marked individuality, differing almost totally from the other races, while showing the most marked affinities among themselves. It would be inappropriate to burden the present sketch with a lengthy dissertation on the peculiarities of the Bantu languages. The most marked feature is the euphonic concord, a principle by which the characteristic prefix of the noun is attached to the pronouns and adjectives qualifying it, and to the verb of which it is the subject. Thus "*Ma*tadi *ma*ma *ma*mpwena *ma*mpembe *me*jitanga beni:" "These great white stones are very heavy." Quoting J. R. Wilson, Mr. Cust remarks that "the Bantu languages are soft, pliant, and flexible, to an almost unlimited extent. Their grammatical principles are founded on the most systematic and philosophical basis, and the number of words may be multiplied to an almost indefinite extent. They are capable of expressing all the nicer shades of thought and feeling, and perhaps no other languages of the world are capable of more definiteness and precision of expression. Livingstone justly remarks that a complaint of the poverty of the language is often only a sure proof of the scanty attainments of the complainant. As a fact the Bantu languages are exceedingly rich." My own researches fully confirm these remarks. The question is vary naturally raised, Whence do these savages possess so fine a language? Is it an evolution now in process from something ruder and more savage, or from something inarticulate? The marked similarity of the dialects points to a common origin; their richness, superiority, and the regularity of the individual character maintained over so large an area, give a high idea of the original language which was spoken before they separated.

Heathenism is degrading, and under its influence everything is going backwards. We are led by the evidence of the language to look for a better, nobler origin of the race, rather than to consider it an evolution from something much lower. The Bantu languages are as far removed from others of the continent as English is from Turkish or Chinese. Some earlier writers have endeavored to trace similarities, but later research has proved that they do not exist. The origin of the race must ever remain a mystery.* What, when, and where, cannot be ascertained, for no memorials exist in books or monuments. The Bantu race and languages cannot be an evolution from something inferior; they are a degradation from something superior. Coastwards there are traditions of change and movement on the part of the people; in the east and on the south marauding tribes and slave hunters have devastated large tracts of country, but there is no sign of general movement on the part of the Bantus.

The traditions of countries along the coast where white men have long settled speak of much greater, more powerful, kingdoms in the past; and after due allowance has been made for exaggeration, it is too evident that the kings of Kongo, Kabinda, Loango, and Angola, exerted at one time far more influence than they do to-day. Indeed, the king of Kongo is the only chief who maintains his style and title;

---

*Why is it not more reasonable to trace its origin back to the tower of Babel and the confounding of tongues by the power of God?—ED.

the others have become extinct during this century. We find, then, the whole country in a state of disintegration, every town a separate state, and its chief, to all practical purposes, independent.

Makoko, the Teke chief with whom De Brazza made his famous treaty, is said to have levied taxes on the north-bank people near his town. The king of Kongo used to receive a tribute from the remnants of the old Kongo empire; but to-day he has to content himself with levying a mild blackmail on passing caravans, and receives a present, when he gives the "hat" and the insignia of office to those who succeed to chieftainships over which, in olden times, the kings exercised control. Few, indeed, of those acknowledge him to-day even to that extent.

These independent townships group themselves into tribes and tribelets; it is, however, a matter of great difficulty to learn the tribal names, which are best obtained from neighbors. The old Kongo empire formerly included the countries on the south bank from the coast to Stanley Pool, and southward to the Buda-speaking people of Ngola (Angola), while homage was rendered by the kings of Loango and Kabinda. To-day the influence of the king is merely nominal outside his town. He is respected, however, in a radius of thirty or forty miles, but seldom, if ever, interferes in any matters.

San Salvador is situated on a plateau one thousand seven hundred feet above the sea, about two and a half miles long by one mile wide. Broad valleys three hundred feet deep surround it, and in the south flows the little river Lueji, a tributary of the Lunda-Mpozo.

There are abundant traces of the former importance of this town. The ruins of a stone wall, two feet thick and fifteen feet high, encircle it. The ruins of the cathedral are very interesting, and show it to have been a very fine building. The material is an ironstone conglomerate, while the lime was burnt from rock in the neighborhood.

Amid the strong, rich grass that covers the plateau exist ruins of some twenty-six buildings, which are said to have been churches, while straight lines of *mingomena* bushes mark the sites of suburban villas and hamlets. The story runs that the old kings kept up the population of the *mbanza* (chief town) by raids into the country. The natives of a town forty miles away would wake up in the morning to find themselves surrounded. As they came out of their houses, they would be killed, until there was no further show of resistance; then those who remained would be deported to the capital and be compelled to build there, while many would be sold to the slave traders on the coast. These days are forever past. Men-of-war have so closely watched the coast that the slave trade has languished and died, except in Angola, where it exists under a finer name, the slave being considered a "Colonial," while Portuguese ingenuity and corruption arrange for "emigration" to the islands of San Thomé, Principe, and even to the Bissagos.

While these slave raids in Kongo are in the main things of the past, a mild domestic slavery exists among the natives. In most cases the slaves are more like feudal retainers or serfs. A man of means invests his money in slaves, and thereby becomes more independent, for his slave retainers can support him in difficulties with his neighbors. It frequently happens that he builds a stockade at a little distance from the town in which he has been brought up, and this becomes the nucleus of a new town. In the latter end of the rainy season and the beginning of the "dries," they will cut *nianga* grass, the long six-foot blades of which spring up out of the ground, and have no stem or nodes. This grass is dried and used for the covering of the huts. Stems of palm fronds are also trimmed and split. Papyrus is brought from the marshes, and strips of its green skin twisted into string, with which they tie together securely the posts and rafters, so that they may stand the strain of the fierce tornadoes which sweep the country.

Rev. David Charters, the missionary quoted in a previous chapter, has this to say about the native inhabitants:—

"One of the most promising and encouraging features of our work in Africa is the simplicity of the people of the interior. You try to strike a bargain with them, and you will find that they are as sharp and perhaps sharper than you are; but in many other respects they are like big children. True it is that they are somewhat prejudiced in favor of their charms; but such prejudices are not nearly so strong as some imagine. It has been my conviction all along,—and still is, and what I have seen has strengthened and deepened that conviction,—that wherever the gospel of Jesus Christ has been preached in sincerity, souls have been converted to God; and, better still, lives have borne testimony to the genuineness of such conversion. Compare the Africans of the coast with the Africans of the interior. In the interior we find wild, unsophisticated children of nature; on the coast we have a set of people who have acquired the vices and evils of the white man, with few of his virtues. They have been contaminated by coming into contact with ungodly and unprincipled men. They have been made ten times worse than they would have been if left alone."

Another important and reliable testimony in reference to the inhabitants of Central Africa is that of Fannie Roper Feudge, of which the following is an extract:—

"One at all familiar with the condition and appearance of the mass of boys and girls in the mission regions before the coming of the missionaries would scarcely recognize them now, so wonderfully have they changed. Many of the children who are now regular pupils in the mission schools had been stolen from their homes by the Arab slave dealers, and when rescued were set down in squads of women and children in some unsettled grove, with little food and clothing, and no shelter except such booths or huts as they were able to make for themselves. Their miserable huts were not sufficiently high to permit them to stand erect, and their only beds were piles of leaves or dried grass; and they had become so utterly disheartened by misfortunes and ill-treatment that few of them had either energy or intellect to struggle into a better life.

"Not only the rescued slaves, but nearly all the people of Central Africa, have been found sunken in ignorance and sin, debased in their lives, gross in their tastes, and wholly destitute of any means of moral or intellectual development. About the only skill or energy manifest was that shown in barricading their dwellings and villages against their enemies and in making aggressions on their neighbors; for with the native African war is the business of life, and the warrior who can show the largest number of skulls of his human victims is the man entitled to the highest respect, and becomes an object of envy among all his countrymen."

Any sketch of the Kongo people would be incomplete without reference to one of its most prominent representatives. Although not a native of that region, he has been so long a resident, and so thoroughly identified with its institutions, as to be a considerable factor in the make-up of the country.

The person to whom we refer is popularly known as Tippu Tib. His real name, says Mr. Herbert Ward, in *Christian at Work*, is Hamed-ben-Mohammad,—Tippu Tib being a nickname given to him on account of a peculiar motion of his eyes. His father was a Zanzibar Arab, and his mother a Mrima negress. He is at present near fifty years of age, and is the owner of extensive plantations and thousands of slaves. He is also an ivory merchant, by which business he has amassed great wealth. His principal residence is at Nyangure, on the Lualaba, or Upper Kongo.

All the travelers, from Livingstone to those of the present day, have had the utmost confidence in Tippu Tib, and he has all along enjoyed a high reputation for fidelity, ability, and courage, and especially for his great hospitality. His great wealth and acknowledged executive ability have won for him extended influence, and he is practically monarch of the region where he operates. It is said that his subjects and slaves are very proud of his exploits.

The name of Tippu Tib came prominently before the civilized world through his connection with Mr. Stanley's last African expedition. He furnished the carriers for the expedition, his contract being for six hundred. In 1877 he had been simply a conductor of caravan for Mr. Stanley, but in the succeeding ten years had become a man of much greater importance. In addition to his wealth, and fame as a trader and planter, he had been honored by the Kongo Free State Government with the appointment of commissioner of the Stanley Pool district. In the last expedition, Major Bartelott, an English officer, was assigned to the command of Stanley's rear column, the chief of the expedition going with the advance. The rear column utterly failed in its part of the great work, and the major and his friends endeavored to lay the blame largely on Tippu Tib, who, it was asserted, failed to fulfill his contract to supply carriers. However, this is a dispute which it is not the province of this book to settle.

Rev. David A. Day contributes the following quaint explanation of African expressions to the *Lutheran Missionary Journal:*—

"After living awhile among these people, we cannot fail to notice the efforts of these languages to provide from their own resources names for new objects which may be brought to their notice. An umbrella is, literally translated, a 'sun ketch' or a 'rain ketch;' captain, a 'canoe king;' steamer, a 'smoke canoe;' school, a 'book place;' spectacles, 'look things;' bell, a 'bam bam;' pantaloons, 'leg cloth;' and rum, 'hot water.'

"Africans have but few abstract ideas, and, like all uncivilized people, have no words to express actions of the mind. Identified so closely with nature, they see in any mental process only a reflection of the world about them, and therefore express themselves almost entirely by the use of figures and parables, some of which are very striking and exceedingly rich. To speak to these people intelligibly one must understand thoroughly these peculiar expressions and be very familiar with their modes of thought. The following literal translations will give an idea of the every-day utterances of our natives.

"'Staff talk,' a name given to the speeches made by anyone in a court of justice, the speaker always holding a staff, which is handed him when his turn comes. When he is through, it is passed back to the presiding officer, who gives it to the next whose turn it may be to take the floor, but who dare not open his mouth until he has the stick; a practice which, if adopted in our church assemblies and legislative halls, would save the president much annoyance and avoid the confusion so often seen at places of that kind.

"'One-leg talk.' When they are pressed for time, the speaker is often made to stand on one leg, and is only to have the floor as long as he can keep that position. A witness may be dealt with in the same way, especially when inclined to be too talkative. Audiences and congregations at home may take a hint from this, and the rule be applied to long-winded orators.

"'Put our hands in cold water' expresses the manner of making peace, all the parties at variance immersing their hands at the same time in a large vessel of cold water, of which each one must then take a drink.

"'Put a log in the path,' to hinder a person by placing obstacles in his way. 'Hands left up,' denying a man's plea for mercy. 'Heart lay down,' pleased; 'heart get up,' frightened; 'we drink the same water,' we are at peace; 'hard-headed,' stubborn; 'woman-hearted' is timid, and when a man likes to boast, he is said to have the 'big-head.' Thunder is 'sky talk,' and the crowing of a rooster is 'chicken talk.'

"The point or edge of any iron instrument is its 'mouth,' as the spear mouth, ax mouth, gun mouth, etc. A man said to me last week when he struck his ax on a rock, 'Daddy, dat ax he mouf done bust.' When a man talks to the point he is said to have 'a sharp mouth,' and when he tells what may get him into trouble, he has 'spoiled his mouth.' Anyone talking too much has a 'long mouth,' while the flatterer has a 'sweet mouth.' Goods that have been stolen are said to have 'gotten feet.' One of the principal duties of the wife is to warm water for the evening bath of the husband, hence marriage is called a 'hot-water concern'—a term which might often be applied in other countries than Africa. The only division of time is that of moons, which are generally named from some peculiarity of the weather at that season or the appearance of the sky. January is the 'big cool moon,' because of the cool nights; February, the 'big smoke moon.' Then there is the 'sky-talk moon,' when it thunders, and the 'foot-track moon,' because of the mud.

"It is quite easy to understand how men with no literature, none of the arts and sciences, and who have always been cut off from other parts of the world, fall into these peculiar expressions. Without our printed and written language, how long would it be before one section of the country could not understand the other? Even as it is, the idioms and peculiar expressions of one State must be acquired by the strangers from another."

CHAPTER V.

HOME LIFE ON THE KONGO.

PERHAPS the home life of the inhabitants of the Kongo Valley may be best shown if some familiar scenes are described.

While engaged in the transport service of the mission, I was sitting quietly in my tent in Sadi Kiandunga's town, when, without the least warning, a volley was fired at less than a hundred yards from my little camp. The men shouted, the women screamed, the wildest commotion ensued. Was it an attack upon the town? What had happened? As a man ran past the tent, I inquired the cause.

"Oh, nothing!" he said; "it is only a baby born, and everyone is glad and shouting out their joy at the safe birth; they have fired a *feu-de-joie*. Don't you do so in your country?"

The house where the little stranger had arrived was very small; a fire was burning inside, filling it with strong wood smoke; and as if there were not sufficient discomfort for such a time, the house was literally crammed with women, all shouting vociferously, showing in this well-meaning but mistaken manner their sympathy in the mother's joy.

The people rise at daybreak, and the fire, which has been kept smouldering all night, is replenished, or, if it has gone out, fire is obtained from another household. The wife clears up the ashes from the hearth, and sweeps out the chips and husks that remain from last night's supper.

MANNER OF DRESSING THE HAIR.

The husband, if a tidy man, sweeps his compound. Negro toilet operations then ensue. A calabash of water is taken behind the house, and, filling his mouth with water, Ndualu (Dom Alvaro) allows a thin stream to flow over his hands as he carefully washes them, also his face; then, cleaning his teeth, he goes to sit in front of his house to comb his hair. The ladies have been bestirring themselves, and a morsel of food is ready—a few roast ground-nuts, or a piece of prepared cassava.

The infants are placed in the care of older babies, and the women and girls of the town wend their way to the village spring, where they bathe and gossip until, all the calabashes being full, they return with the day's supply of water. One calabash is for the baby, who is brought outside and carefully washed, squalling lustily as the cold douche is poured over him. If the mother is careful, his feet are examined for jiggers. This sand flea, brought from Brazil some twenty years ago, is a great pest. Burrowing into the feet, often in the most tender parts, the insect swells until its eggs are mature, when the little cist, or sack, bursts, and they are set free. If they are not extracted, the jiggers set up an inflammation, which may even terminate in mortification. It is very common to see one or two toes absent from this cause.

The preliminaries of the day being over, the women start for the farms. Taking with them in the great conical basket a hoe, a little food, and a small calabash of water, the baby is carried on the hip, or more often made to straddle its mother's back, and tied on with a cloth dexterously fastened in front. So the poor child travels, often through the hot sun, bound tightly to its mother's reeking body, its little head but inadequately protected by its incipient wool. No wonder that an African baby who has survived the hardships of babyhood grows up to be strong and able to bear great strain and fatigue. The weaklings are early weeded out, and often poor mothers, wringing their hands, wail and deplore the loss of the little darling, whose death is due to their own lack of care, rather than to the supposed witchcraft and devilish malice of someone in the town.

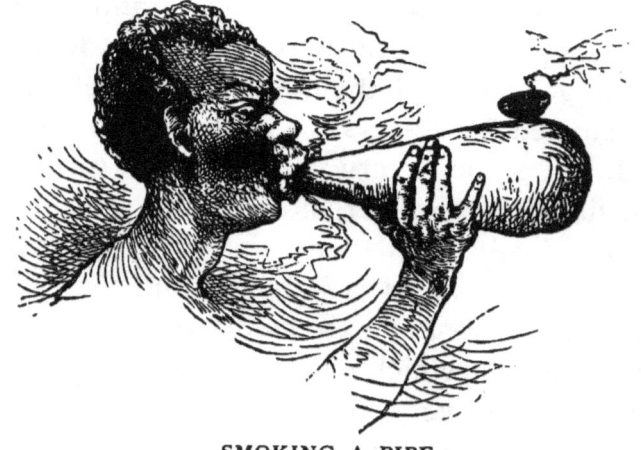

SMOKING A PIPE.

The men will sometimes help in the farms when trees have to be felled, but otherwise the women perform the farm work; and as the ground does not need much scratching to produce a crop, the hoeing and weeding afford them healthful employment, sufficient to keep them so far out of mischief. We have seen towns in the neighborhood of Stanley Pool where the women do no farm work, living on the proceeds of their husband's ivory trade; they gossip, smoke, sleep, and cook, or spend an hour or two in arranging the coiffure of their lord or of a companion. Laziness is not good for any people, and where there is so little housework the gardening is not too severe a tax on the women. Towards evening they return, bringing some cabbage or cassava leaves, or something to make up some little relish, and proceed to cook the evening meal. The men have their own departments of work. They are great traders.

The Kongo week consists of four days, Nkandu, Konzo, Nhenge, Nsona, and every four or eight days they hold their markets. As they have many markets within a moderate distance, and occurring on different days of the week, there is generally a market to attend on each day, if anyone is so disposed. The market-places are in open country, generally on a hilltop, away from towns. These precautions prevent surprises.

On the appointed day large numbers of men, women, and children are to be met carrying their goods. There is cassava in various forms, dried, in puddings, or as meal; plantain, ground-nuts, and other food-stuffs; pigs, goats, sheep, fowls, and fish; dried caterpillars on skewers; dried meat; wares from Europe, such as cloth, beads, knives, guns, brass wire, salt, gunpowder. Palm wine, native beer, sometimes gin and rum are found in abundance. Native produce, such as palm oil, ground-nuts, sesamum, india rubber, crates of fowls, bundles of native cloth, meal sieves, baskets, hoes, etc., are also found in these markets.

Stringent laws are made to protect the markets. No one is allowed to come armed, no one may catch a debtor on market day, no one may use a knife against another in a passion. The penalty for all these offenses is death, and many muzzles of buried guns stick up in the market-places to warn other rowdies against a like fate. Between the coast and Stanley Pool beads are the currency; above the pool brass rods take their place. A man wishing to sell salt and to buy india rubber, first sells his salt for beads, and with the beads buys the rubber. Large profits can be made in these markets, and many natives spend the greater part of their time traveling from one to another for the purpose of trade.

Children commence trading very early. A five-year-old boy will somehow get three or four strings of beads, and with them will buy a small chicken. After a few months of patient care, it is worth eight or ten strings, and his capital is doubled. He is soon able to buy a small pig, which follows him about like a dog, and sleeps in his house, until, by and by, it fetches a good amount on the market. The proceeds of rat hunting, barter among the town boys, and further trade, have meanwhile increased his stock in trade. When he grows older, he accompanies a caravan to the coast; he gets a nice present to carry food for his uncle; on his way to and from the coast his ideas of trade are enlarged. He commences to buy india rubber, and brings back with him next time salt and cloth, a gun and some powder, a knife and a plate. And so by degrees he is encouraged to fresh effort, until he has sufficient to pay for a wife or two. Continuing still in trade, he buys and sells, investing his property in slave retainers, and hiding some in reserve, in case of misfortune, or against his death, that he may be buried in a large quantity of cloth. It is a great ambition among all to be thus buried. You will hear it said that so and so was buried, and that he was wound in two hundred fathoms of cloth, and that fifty guns were buried with him, and so on. The Kongo natives consider this as great a privilege as an Englishman would to be buried in Westminster Abbey.

The girls help their mothers in farming and housework until they arrive at a marriageable age. In some places they are betrothed very early, the intended husband paying a deposit, and by installments completing the price demanded by the girl's maternal relatives. The amount is often heavy—reckoned by Kongo wealth—but varies much according to the position of the girl's family or the suitor's wealth. It is altogether a business matter. Should the wife die, her maternal relatives have to provide another wife without further payment; and as frequently they have spent the sum paid in the first instance, they are landed in difficulties. "Palavers," or conferences and disagreements about women are a fruitful source of war.

Children are considered the property of the wife's

relatives; the father has little or no control over them. The right of inheritance is from uncle to nephew, thus a man's slaves and real property go to the eldest son of his eldest sister, or the next of kin on such lines. A wise nephew will therefore leave his father's house, and go to live with his uncle, whom he hopes to succeed. His uncle, also, knowing that his nephew is to inherit his goods, while his own children belong to his wife's clan, cares more for his nephew than his own children. The evil of the system is recognized by many, but they cannot see how the necessary revolution is to be brought about.

At the age of five or six the boys do not stay longer with their mothers. Some bigger boys having built a house, the small boys just breaking loose from parental restraints go to them, and beg to be allowed to live with them. They in turn promise to find them in firewood, and to be their little servants for the time being. These boys' houses are called *mbonge*. I turned up late at night (eight o'clock) in a native town, having made a forced march. I had never visited there before, and not liking to rouse the chief at such an hour, I went to the *mbonge*, and asked the boys whether my two attendants and I might sleep there to save trouble, as I must be off again at daybreak. "Oh, you are Ingelezo [English], are you? Come in. Yes, we are glad to see you, so often we have heard of you, and now we see you. We are very pleased." This was kindly spoken; so, stooping through the low doorway, I entered a roomy house. Some ten boys had just finished supper, and squatted round a smoky fire. I was glad to stretch out on the papyrus mat they gave me, keeping low down to avoid the smoke, which otherwise almost blinded me. I had with me half a fowl, a small bell worth about three cents, and three strings of beads. A boy spitted my fowl over the fire, while my attendants dozed, for they were worn out with the long march of the day. I begged some plantain, and a lad went to the door and shouted, "Bring some plantain to the *mbonge.*" A kindly woman brought some. When my meal was ready, I asked for a pinch of salt and some water; they shouted for these, and got them. Having finished my meal, I coiled up in my blanket. Next morning, giving them the bell and three strings, I thanked them, and so we parted.

The boys of the *mbonge* are well attended to by the people of the village; for to get the name of "stingy" is the first step towards the terrible rumor of witch.

The constant activities of trade tend to develop the intellectual faculties of the people. There are many sharp, long-headed men, who, having no account books or invoices, possess wonderful memories and ask you many sensible questions; and if you can speak their language, an hour's chat with them may be as pleasant as with some whiter and more civilized people. If you wish to make a bargain with them, you need all your wits and firmness; for if they are stronger than you, or have no reason to respect you, they are sure to have their way.

They are possessed of much constructive skill. They are clever in the manufacture of pottery and metal work; they make hoes and knives, cast bracelets, anklets, and even bells from the brass rods of trade, and beat out brass wire and ribbon. They strike you at once as being savages of a superior type.

We might draw another picture. There are some districts where there seems to be no energy in the people. Take, for instance, the Majinga or the Lukunga Valley, as we knew them some time ago. Here the natives live in the midst of plenty, for the soil is not to be equaled in richness. The proceeds of a goat sold on one of the markets will supply a large family with palm-fiber cloth for a year, while a crate or two of fowls will provide salt, gunpowder, and an occasional hoe or plate.

A boy grows up in this rich country, and for a while his intellect expands as he learns about the little world around him. As he grows older, he may bestir himself to find means to buy a gun, and then a wife; but, that accomplished, he has practically nothing more to learn or live for. He sleeps or smokes all day, unless perhaps about September, when the grass is burnt and there is a little hunting, though a war or a palaver may sometimes break the monotony. Otherwise, his wife cultivates the land and feeds him; he eats and sleeps. Living such an animal life, his intellect stagnates, and he becomes quarrelsome and stupid to a degree almost hopeless. He is dirty and indolent, and is contented to see his hut fall to pieces almost over his head.

The women are often satisfied with but a rag for clothing. Their adornments are still more curious. They wear a grass stem three inches long through the nose, and a dirty rag for an earring. The hair is matted with a mixture of oil and vegetable charcoal; and if a woman happens to be in mourning, the same filthy compound is smeared over her face.

The public roads are simply footpaths, somewhat similar to those made by the American Indians. Some of them are very old, having been traveled over for centuries. They are so worn down in many places as to resemble a winding gutter. On rolling ground the rain has helped to wash them out to a greater depth. Mr. Stanley remarks that they are unnecessarily winding, and many times one-third of the distance could have been saved by straighter paths. In this respect they are unlike the American Indian trails, which are always remarkable for their directness of course.

The natives, as a rule, know but little of the country beyond their own immediate surroundings. They do not travel far from home. Of course they are learning more, through being employed by various kinds of expeditions as carriers. But, owing to their superstitions regarding what is beyond their knowledge, it is often difficult to get them to go far outside of their own limited range, and many will desert when confronted with unusual scenes and future uncertainties.

Mr. Stanley tells about starting out on one of his expeditions, having given a native the position of guide. The position of "foremost man" was deemed one of great honor, and the fellow was real proud—"the proudest soul in the column"—and wore a conspicuous headdress. The following short extract from "In Darkest Africa" will illustrate the point:—

"'Which is the way, guide?' I asked.

"'This way, running toward the sunrise,' he replied.

"'How many hours to the next village?'

"'God alone knows,' he answered.

"'Know ye not one village or country beyond here?'

"'Not one. How should I?' he asked.

"'Well, then, set on in the name of God, and God be ever with us. Cling to any track that leads by the river until we find a road.'

"'Bismillah!' echoed the pioneers; the Nubian trumpets blew the signal of 'move on,' and shortly the head of the column disappeared into the thick bush beyond the utmost bounds of the clearings of Yambuya."

CARAVAN CROSSING A RIVER.

With the advent of white men old-time features have begun to change. The Livingstone Inland Mission (American Baptists) and the International Association have stations among them; their transport and that of the Baptist Missionary Society (English) passes through the country. The people are coming forward as carriers; they sell their goats, fowls, etc., and are getting cloth; and in this short time a change for the better is apparent. Here lies all the difference between the degraded and the higher types of the African. The intellect of the one is stagnant, while the other has everything to quicken it.

As children the better class will compare favorably with English boys; bright, sharp, anxious to learn, they push on well with their studies. Our schools are full of promise. At Stanley Pool not long since the boys were much concerned because a new boy had mastered his alphabet the first day. They all felt that he was too clever.

The future of these interesting people is full of the brighest hope. Give them the gospel, and with it the advantages of education, and books to read, quicken within them tastes which will render labor a necessity and a pleasure, give them something high and noble to work and live for, and we shall see great and rapid changes. Christian missions are no experiment. We have to deal with a vigorous race, that will repay all that Christian effort can do on their behalf.

CHAPTER VI.

RELIGIOUS IDEAS OF THE NATIVES.

IT cannot be said that there is a religion throughout the whole region of the Kongo. There is no idolatry, no system of worship; there is nothing but a vague superstition, a groping in blindness; there is the deepest, saddest ignorance and darkness, without a hope of light. The people have the name of God, but know nothing further about him. Their idea is not, however, of an evil being, or they would wish to propitiate him or win his favor. A mild and gentle chief gets little respect or honor. A man who is hard and stern, reckless of life, is feared and respected. Hence, as they fear no evil from God, they do not trouble themselves about him in any way—never even pray to him. Perhaps it may be because they regard him as beyond their reach and knowledge, or think that he is careless of them.

Nzambi, or some slightly modified form, such as Nyambi or Anyambie, is the name by which God is known over the explored regions of the western portion, while the Bayansi of the upper river use also Molongo, which is the same as Mulungu and

Muungu of the east coast. Of the derivation of Nzambi we cannot speak definitely or even approximately. Suffice it to say that the word has a sense of greatness, and conveys a definite idea of a Supreme Being. It cannot be connected with a vague notion of sky, having nothing common with the word "*ezulu*" (heaven).

There is a decided idea of personality, and the Kongos generally speak of Nzambi-ampungu, the Most High (Supreme) God. The name of God is all that they know, and certainly they have no notion of any means of communication between God and man. They regard him as the Creator, and as the sender of rain, but would never under any circumstances think of their voice being heard in heaven. So, having no helper, they betake themselves to charms to avert evil and for general protection.

The knowledge of the name of God gives us a good means by which to reach them. We can tell them that we bring them a message from Nzambi himself, not a story of a white man's God, but their God and ours, and at once we get a ready and deeply-interested hearing.

"Have you seen Nzambi?" "Does he live in the white man's land under the sea?" "How did you hear this news?" Such are the questions they are ever ready to ask.

On one occasion, at Stanley Pool, a lad from the far upper river sold by Zombo traders to the

Bayansi, asked me: "But, Mundele, all joking apart, what do you really come here for if you do not want to trade? Tell me truly." I told him that we had been commissioned with the message of good news from Nzambi, and that was our real and sole business. "What! Nzambi, who lives in the heavens (Nzambi kun' ezulu)?" As he said this, he pointed up into the sky. Poor boy! I wondered how he knew that there was a God, and that he so instinctively pointed up to the blue sky. I saw him once or twice after that. He soon returned to his distant home, but could tell his people that he had seen white men, who were coming soon to bring them a good message from Nzambi.

They have a very decided idea of a future state, but as to what and where, the opinion is much divided. Indeed, there is not the remotest notion that death can be a cessation of being. If anyone dies, they think that someone, living or dead, has established a connection with the unseen world, and somehow, and for some purpose, has "witched away" the deceased.

When a man is sick, he first resorts to bleeding and simple remedies. If no relief is obtained, a native doctor is called. The man's friends and relatives help him to pay the fee, if large. Having agreed as to the fee, the doctor may fetch aromatic or bitter leaves from the woods, and make a decoction of them, wring them in water, or in some way extract their properties. Perhaps he may add a small scraping of a snake's head, of a few nuts or seeds, or of some mysterious articles in his bundle of charms. There is an endless variety of things which their superstition prompts them to do.

Mr. Comber was recently watching a "doctoring" at Ngombe. A chief, Lutete, was sick, and the people were very anxious about him. The doctor called for a fowl, a string was tied to its leg, and the other end to Lutete's arm. After some mysterious actions, and placing some white marks with pipeclay upon the body of the sufferer, he proceeded to push the complaint from the extremities into the body, from the body into the arm, and finally succeeded in drawing the disease down the arm, through the string, and into the unfortunate fowl, which doubtless was little the worse for its vicarious position, until the doctor had it killed for his evening meal.

There is far more knavery than skill in all their doctoring. If the disease does not yield to such treatment, other doctors are called in; and as matters become more serious, they consider that it is evidently not a simple case of sickness, for it will not yield to skillful physicians; it must be a case of witchcraft. The sufferer now becomes terribly anxious, and nganga-a-moko (the charms doctor) is called in. His duty is to tell what and why the patient ails. He may say that it is a simple sickness, and prescribe accordingly. Or, if he deems it really serious, he declares it to be a case of witchcraft.

He professes to be able to ascertain who is "witching" the sufferer; but as it is not his business to mention names, he does not do so, neither do people inquire. Having made thorough diagnosis, he shouts to the witch, who is spoken of as nximbi (pronounced *n'-shim-bi*), to let his patient alone, to let him live. "Does he not know that this wicked course will bring its desserts? If he persists in destroying his victim, the witch doctor will surely find him out." Then all the people join in calling upon the unknown nximbi to relinquish his victim. The agony of mind of the sufferer, and of those dear to him, can be imagined.

If, in spite of all, the man dies, in grief and rage the family call for the witch doctor, nganga-a-ngombo. Space prevents a detailed description of his methods of procedure. He is a cunning rogue, and has his secret agent, who ascertains whether anyone is in special disfavor, or whom it will be safe to declare a witch. He may decide haphazard, or he may ascertain that the deceased man dreamed of someone. He consults nganga-a-moko. At early dawn the sound of his ding-winti drum startles the town. Who knows whether he may not be accused of the crime?

After working people into the wildest frenzy by a protracted series of dances and mystery, the doctor at last selects one or two of those present, and declares him or them to be guilty of the devilish crime. The excitement culminates; the victim declares his innocence and ignorance; but the rascally doctor tells a long story of the way in which the crime was accomplished, till all feel the guilt fully established, and would like to tear the witch to pieces on the spot. However, there is a regular course of things to pass through before the individual is condemned. He must take the ordeal poison, and a market day is appointed when this shall be done. On the day decided, all the people of the district assemble in vast crowds, as they used to do in England before executions were performed in private.

The poor victim believes his innocence will be established, and fearfully, but still generally willingly, he drinks the poisonous draught. His stomach may reject the noxious compound. If he vomits, the man is declared innocent, and the witch doctor loses his fee—indeed, in some parts he is heavily fined for a false charge. More often, if he has not avoided the risk by referring the death to some charm, or to some person recently dead, he does his work too surely. His victim staggers and falls. With a wild yell the bystanders rush at him and beat him to death, shoot him, burn or bury him alive, throw him over a precipice, or in some way finish the terrible work, with a savage ferocity equal to their deep sense of the enormity of the crime with which he is charged.

One could gather hundreds of terrible stories of the like kind, with much variety of detail; but the same principle runs through all. We heard of a case where, on the nganga making his declaration, the witch man went into his house close by, fetched his gun, and shot the witch doctor dead on the spot. He had to pay twenty slaves to the friends of the nganga, but no one ventured further to trouble that witch.

Sometimes, and in some places, the witch doctor is called in in case of sickness only, and witches are killed to stay the sickness; and again he is called at the death of the person, sometimes even in the case of a baby's death. A serious accident—as drowning, a fall from a palm tree, or the death of a chief—is considered the work of several witches; one alone could not accomplish such a thing. Six men of the Vivi towns were drowned through the upsetting of a canoe in the rapids, and three witches were found for each man; eighteen victims had to suffer for the death of those six men—twenty-four deaths in all.

Even when the victim vomits, and should be free, they sometimes find an excuse to finish the work.

"But why," you ask, "did you kill Mpanzu? What did he do to the man who died? Did anyone see him do it?"

"O Mundele! why do you ask such questions? Did not nganga-a-ngombo ascertain by his witch charms? Did he not tell us how he did it? And when he took the ordeal and swooned, was not his guilt proved? Why, we should all say that anyone who dared to question such a decision must be himself a witch!"

"But what does a witch do—how does he do it?"

"How do I know? I am not a witch. Why, if we did not kill our witches, we should all die in no time! What would check them?"

You cannot get much further than this with young people or common folk; all accept the word of the nganga without question. Indeed, many of them have been accused, and have been fortunate enough to reject the poison. Those who may escape by vomiting the draught are generally confirmed in the truthfulness of the ordeal that established their innocence. However, I have never discussed the matter privately with an intelligent native who did not acknowledge the wickedness and deplore the custom. The fear of being dubbed a witch compels generosity, and here lies the strength of the custom.

Nga Mbelenge, one of the chiefs of the district of Leopoldville, Stanley Pool, has told me how it fared with him.

"I had a town of my own when quite young. You know how the Bayansi sell to the Bakongo, and we act as middlemen, and interpret for them. I pushed business, and many traders came to me because they had so much trouble with the other old chiefs about here. I soon became very rich, married several wives, bought many slaves out of my profits, and my town grew large.

"The other old chiefs, instead of pushing their trade, grumbled that I got so much. They would say: 'Look at young Nga Mbelenge; how rapidly he is growing rich! It seems only yesterday he was a boy, and now to-day look at his town, see how rich he is! No doubt he is selling souls also.' Without any warning or trial, they came down on me suddenly, accused me of witchcraft, and in my own town compelled me to drink the ordeal poison. I vomited, and thus my innocence was established." He acknowledged that the whole custom is very wicked. "But what am I to do? If I say that I will have no more of it in my town, my people will say that I am myself a witch, and therefore I do not wish further execution for witchcraft. If I try to stop it, I bring it upon myself."

As a sequel to this, I learned that a fortnight after, another man was killed in his town as a witch.

The question is naturally asked, What is this crime of witchcraft? Those people who do any trading imagine that a witch is able by means of some fell sorcery to possess himself of the spirit of his victim. He can then put the spirit into a tusk of ivory, or among his merchandise, and convey it to the coast, where the white men will buy it. In due course, if not at the time, the "witched" man dies. Then the white man can make him work for him in his country under the sea. They believe that very many of the coast laborers are men thus obtained, and often when they go to trade, look anxiously about for dead relatives. Sometimes when we are traveling, they look on with wonder and disgust as we open our canned provisions, "calculating" that that at least must be one of the uses to which we put their dead relatives.

The notion of the land under the sea has its origin in their faculty of observation. They see that ships coming from sea appear, first the mast, then the hull; and thus at a decent distance out, so as not to reveal the trick, we white men seem to emerge from the ocean. Travelers love to enlarge upon the wonders they have seen, and so the story grows, and the people have been brought up in the belief that away under the sea their relatives make cloth, etc., for us white people.

This is, however, a new idea, comparatively. The old notion still prevails in many parts that away in some dark forest land departed spirits dwell. The witches, they think, have some interest in sending away their fellows to the spirit land. Perhaps they get pay from the spirits, no one knows or questions why. Who can know a witch's business but a witch?

Even if a man dies in war, or is taken by a wild beast or crocodile, it is witchcraft. To such an extent is this believed that people will bathe in streams where crocodiles abound. So long as there are plenty of people together, the cowardly reptiles are not likely to attack. In this way the idea has come about that real crocodiles will not eat men; but if such a thing occurs, it is proof positive that either a witch has transformed himself into a crocodile to obtain his victim, or induced the reptile to do it for him. If you ask how, the answer is, "I do not know; I am not a witch." At Lukunga, Mr. Ingham, of the Livingstone Mission, shot a huge crocodile which came out at night after his pigs. In the stomach of the reptile were the anklets of a woman, which were at once recognized by the townsfolk. Yet they told me that the crocodile could not have eaten the woman.

"But how about those anklets?"

"Very likely crocodiles have a fancy for such things. You see what a lot of stones he had in his stomach. Perhaps he took off those anklets when he had done as he was told to do."

This was no ghastly joke. I discussed the matter further, and asked a more intelligent companion whether he could really believe as he asserted. He replied that the man was not joking.

A lad who was for some time a scholar at our school at Underhill Station, died in his own town a month or two after leaving us. The people said that our Mr. Hughes had stolen the boy's soul, and sent it away to the white man's land to be converted into Krooboys to work for us.

The Ngombe people told us that once on the market near their town some travelers halted to buy palm wine, and all the people heard a hoarse voice proceed from a tusk of ivory, "Give me a drink of wine, I am fearfully thirsty." Some wine was poured into the tusk, there was a sound of drinking, and after rest the travelers passed on. Everyone believed the story, but I could never see anyone who was present. It was of course believed to be a spirit on the way to the coast.

Witch doctors are up to all manner of tricks in their wicked business. Sometimes they declare that a dead man is the witch, and will dig in the grave, and as they get near the corpse, suddenly tell the people to get out of the way, the doctor is going to shoot the witch; then, throwing down a little blood which he has secreted, he fires a gun and points triumphantly to the blood of the escaped witch.

One of our boys told us how he had helped to unmask one of these tricks. His mother was ill, and the doctor said that there was a witch in the ground under the head of the bed on which she slept. The people all went out of the house; but the boy, who was anxious to witness the destruction of the witch, begged to remain, and while the doctor was busy digging, he found a bundle under the bed, and took it out. It was the doctor's charms, and among them he found the gizzard of a fowl full of blood. He took it to the chief, who examined it, and the doctor, discovering his loss, came out to say that the witch had been too sharp for him. He was obliged to run away, the people were so angry with him for trying thus to deceive them. It might seem too much to believe that, once discovered, he would venture the same trick again; yet some time after, he was sent to inquire as to the death of a man in the town, and declared that there were two witches, one he pointed out, the other was a dead man. He proceeded to dig up the dead witch, and the chief, remembering at once the old dodge of this very man, sent someone to fetch his bundle, which he was more carefully watching. There was another gizzard ready. This was too much for them. They seized the wretched man, and, breaking his arms and legs, threw him over the precipice, the fate intended for his victim.

There is a story which explains the cruelty of breaking the arms and legs. A man had been accused of witchcraft, and thrown down into the great chasm, a distance of over one hundred feet. He fell into some soft mud at the bottom, and was able the next day to return to the town. The people then broke his arms and legs to make sure of him, and threw him down again; and such is now the course pursued toward like criminals.

Witch stories without end there are, but they still leave unsolved the question, What is a witch? Some say a man who knows how to weave the spell, that is, to throw such influences around a person as will injure or destroy him in spite of all he may do. Others say that an evil spirit takes up its abode in a man to accomplish his ruin. In either case, it is held to be an imperative duty to kill the men. The spirit world is either under the sea or in a dark forest land; but how the spirits live, and what they do, is not known, since no one has ever returned to tell the story. But ghouls and evil spirits are said to lurk about in the neighborhood of graves and uncanny places.

There is a natural fear of death—the spirit world is an unknown land—but there is no apprehension of meeting Nzambi, nor is there a burden of sin.

There is a sense of right and wrong. To steal, to lie, or to commit other crimes is considered wrong, but only a wrong to those who suffer thereby—there is no thought of having sinned against God.

CHAPTER VII.

CANNIBALISM, FREEMASONRY, AND CHARMS.

CANNIBALISM is not met with on the Kongo until we ascend almost to Stanley Pool. The first tribe of the Bateke—the Alali—on the north bank are said to eat human flesh sometimes, but only those who have been killed for witchcraft. The Amfuninga, or Amfunu, the next tribe of Bateke, are also credited with the same horrible vice. It is only a report; we have no evidence of the fact. From Bolobo (two degrees south latitude) upwards it is known to be a custom. White men have had to witness the cutting up of victims, being powerless to prevent the act. When remonstrated with, the natives have replied, "You kill your goats, and no one finds fault with you; let us kill our meat then." When eating their ghastly meal, the parents give morsels of the cooked flesh to the little ones, to give them the taste for such food.

Why they eat human flesh it would be difficult to say. Tribes towards the east coast eat their enemies that they may gain their strength and courage, and it is probable that some such notion underlies the custom on the Upper Kongo.*

It is customary on the upper river to bury—sometimes alive—slaves or wives of a deceased chief. This is done that he may not appear without attendants in the spirit world. Truly, as the prophet says, "The dark places of the earth are full of the habitations of cruelty."

There are two customs which prevail through the country—Ndembo, and another, very much like Freemasonry, called Nkimba.

In the practice of Ndembo, the initiating doctors get someone to fall down in a pretended fit, and in this state he is carried away to an inclosed place outside the town. This is called "dying Ndembo." Others follow suit, generally boys and girls, but often young men and women. Most feign the fit; but sometimes, when it has become the fashion, others will be attacked with hysteria, and so the doctor gets sufficient for a wholesale initiation, twenty or thirty, or even fifty.

They are supposed to have died. But the parents and friends supply food, and after a period varying,

---

* The practice of eating human flesh is fast disappearing, especially as the people come in contact with the white race. So far as this contact has been strong enough to make the *power* of civilized nations felt, the custom has been abandoned. Explorers have found that interior tribes which have not known the white man by actual acquaintance have heard of him, and seem to know of his hostility to cannibalism. These tribes, on the approach of an exploring party, if they were very anxious to be friendly, would say that they did not eat men, but that some neighboring tribes did.

according to custom, from three months to three years, it is arranged that the doctor shall bring them to life again. The custom is not only degrading, but extremely mischievous in its results. So bad is it that, before we reached San Salvador, the king of Kongo had stopped the custom in his town, and others had followed suit in neighboring districts, giving the reason that it was too vile to be continued.

When the doctor's fee has been paid, and money (goods) saved for a feast, the Ndembo people are brought to life. At first they pretend to know no one and nothing; they do not even know how to masticate food, and friends have to perform that office for them. They want everything good that anyone uninitiated may have, and beat them if it is not granted, or even strangle and kill people. They do not get into trouble for this, because it is thought that they do not know better. Sometimes they carry on the pretense by talking gibberish, and behaving as if they had returned from the spirit world. After this they are known by another name, peculiar to those who have "died Ndembo." There seems to be no advantage accruing to the initiated, the license and the love of mystery seem to be the only inducements. We hear of the custom far along on the upper river, as well as in the cataract region.

The Nkimba custom is an introduction from the coast of comparatively recent times. An initiatory fee of about two dollars in cloth and two fowls is paid, and the novice repairs to an inclosure outside of the town. He is given a drug which stupefies him, and when he comes to himself, he finds his fellow Nkimbas wearing a crinoline of palm frondlets, their bodies whitened with pipe clay, and speaking a mysterious language. Only males are initiated into this rite, which is more like Freemasonry. Living apart for a period, varying from six months to two years, he acquires the mysterious language, and at the end of his time he is reckoned a full brother, mbwamve anjata, and all Nkimbas in all districts hail him as a brother, help him in his business, give him hospitality, conversing freely with him in the mystic language. It is no gibberish, as that attempted by the Ndembo fraternity, but until quite lately no white man could get any collection of words. I have, however, been able to get over two hundred words and forty sentences; and while still unable to understand thoroughly the principles on which it has been made up, it is evident that it has been made. The vocabulary is limited, and is characterized by the system of alliteral concord. Some words are slight changes of ordinary Kongo, and others bear no resemblance.

The common people are given to understand that the Nkimba know how to catch witches. In the daytime they wander in the grass, and dig for roots, and gather nuts in the woods, often beating people on the roads who do not run away on their approach. At night they rush about screaming and yelling and uttering their wild trill. Woe to the unfortunate man who ventures out of his house in the night for any purpose; a beating and heavy fine will surely follow.

There is no other nonsense to add to the mystery and fear, but the whole *raison d'être* is the establishment of this fraternity, or guild, for mutual help and protection; and the period of separation is for the acquirement of the useful mystic language. Ndembo is an unmitigated abomination; Nkimba is comparatively harmless, and, in the absence of something better, useful. It is making its way in from the coast, and may be found interiorwards on the south bank for one hundred and seventy-five miles.

An instance of the usefulness of Nkimba is supplied in the story of the founding of our Bayneston station. It was decided that a promontory jutting into the river near Vunda would be a more advantageous site for a base of water transport on the piece of river between Isangila and Manyanga. We were then using the wild river there because the road by land was blocked. We had carried overland for fifty miles our steel sectional boat, the Plymouth. Landing on the promontory, Messrs. Comber and Hartland pitched their tents for the night, sending a message to the towns on the hills by a fisherman that they would like to see the chiefs in the morning. Up to eleven o'clock no one appeared, and they determined to go themselves. As they neared the towns, all was in the wildest excitement; no white man had ever been there before. The women had been sent into the woods, and the men advanced in the grass with their guns, to fight the intruders. The missionaries had with them a head man who was a Nkimba, and, seeing the dangerous state of affairs, he rushed forward, uttering the Nkimba trill; this was replied to, and all was quiet. The missionaries were received by some of the principal men, who agreed to let them have the headland, and, a fortnight later, they signed the contract, selling the land to us, in consideration of a fitting present. Some of our best native scholars are called away sometimes to be initiated into Nkimba.

As the natives of the Kongo Basin know of no means of communicating with Nzambi (God), they take to charms. A Kongo boy grows up, and sees everyone with his charms. One man boasts that he has a charm that will make him rich, and he ties to it a little strip of every piece of cloth he buys; others have charms to keep away witches, charms against theft or sickness, to stop or to bring rain, charms which enable them to cure sicknesses, or to perform the office of witch doctor, of nganga-a-moko, or to discover theft. From very babyhood a child hears the word "nkixi" (pronounced *n'-kish-i*) frequently uttered; no wonder, then, that, as he grows up, he thinks that there must be something in it. He knows a man who, for a consideration, will teach him to make a charm, or perhaps will sell him a little image and bundle of mysteries. Fondly hoping that it will do all that the charm doctor has promised, he always keeps it with him, and perhaps believes that his own life is in the thing, and if anyone got possession of it, he could cause his death; he dare not sleep without it near him; and so the falsehood works until he becomes its slave.

I have watched a chief on market day weaving his spells. He would bring out his charms and spread them on a mat, take a little red powder, work it into a paste, and put some on his image and on each side of his own forehead; he would then rummage in his bundles, and find some mysterious nuts, or something strange, scrape a tiny fragment and put it into his mouth, nibble it, and spit and sputter over his image and charms, then take a little gunpowder, and mix a little mystery with it, and burn it on a stone. Next, chewing some colanut, he would spit and sputter it over the charms, burn more powder, rummage further among his charms; and finally, making some marks on his temples and forehead, he would be ready to go to market.

Such a man is feared. Who knows what he could do with all those charms? His air of mystery, the fuss he makes, his boasts—these, with a large amount of knavery, make the common people think him a great man.

CANNIBALISM, FREEMASONRY, AND CHARMS. 95

On one occasion, in the early times of the mission, Mr. Comber was forbidden to sleep in a town on the road. He was compelled to sleep out in the grass with his people without shelter. There was some sign of rain, so the carriers begged one of their number, who boasted much of his rain charms, to avert the coming storm. He worked hard with his charms, but, notwithstanding, it rained hard on the shelterless people nearly all night. The medicine man said that his charms would not work with white men about.

Among our hired laborers from the coast and elsewhere, we have often had in our gangs rascals making much fuss about their charms, and in consequence much feared by all their workfellows. They were consulted by their mates in sickness, and demanded heavy pay for their advice. Then, because they were supposed to have such great powers for evil as well as for good, they would borrow money or goods, and no one dare refuse, or make them repay. They would need to be constantly propitiated, and thus one scoundrel would get eventually a large share of the wages of his mates. We could never get direct evidence or proof, and could not interfere; and as the payments would mostly be made after they had received their wages, and were beyond our reach, we had to know of the evil, but were powerless to check it.

This, however, is more a coast type. Those nearest to "civilization" are far more superstitious, or, rather, make more use of superstitions, than the natives of the interior. But everywhere the same principles work in a variety of forms.

There are, doubtless, many simple folk who believe it all; many must, however, be consciously imposing on their fellows. To-day, even in England and America, there are people who would hesitate to take down the horseshoe which was put up over the doorway "for luck;" others still believe it unlucky to pass under a ladder. Dream charms and fortune telling have not yet disappeared from these enlightened lands.

There is an infinite variety of charms in Kongo; almost everything may go towards their composition,—dry leaves, snakes' heads, hawks' claws, feathers, elephants' skin, stones, seeds, nuts, beans, the horns of the smaller antelopes, but with all a quantity of red ocher. Pipe clay also plays an important part.

Images have been mentioned, not that they are idols, or more personal than bundles of mysteries, but just as children playing with clay would think first of making a little man, so Kongos often make hideous, rudely-carved little images, with, perhaps, a piece of looking-glass on the chest.

In some towns there may be seen a great image under a sheltering roof, which represents the charm that protects the town. Children are placed under its protection by the payment of a fee to the nganga who weaves certain spells and makes certain articles taboo. In some places it is nlongo (taboo) to eat an egg, or a fowl, goat's head, hippopotamus' flesh, pork, yams, antelope flesh, rats, bananas. This taboo must be observed to insure the protection of the fetish; to break it would entail disease and death. Sometimes a town possesses an image charm which will enable its doctor to find out thefts, and in consequence the people are afraid to steal. Talking with a man once about this "thief medicine," he positively declared the truthfulness of the oracle. "Why, I was found out myself once," he said. "I went to Dedede's town, and stole a piece of cloth from a man's house. No one saw me, or had any means of knowing that I did it, and yet the thief doctor found me out at once. What can you say after that?"

Often in the houses of the sick, the "medicine" may be seen in one corner of the room, consisting, perhaps, of a dirty image and charms, bespattered with blood and chewed cola-nut.

So strong is the belief in the discerning power of these charms that a thief will sometimes return what he has stolen rather than incur the disease that might follow. I know a case in which a man lost something in a town. He paid a small fee to the thief doctor, who arranged with his charms to curse the thief with disease if the articles were not restored by the next morning. The things appeared in due course, and were found lying in front of the door, having been returned during the night.

These charms are sometimes addressed and often scolded when they do not act as they ought; but even the images in no way take the places of idols, neither are they regarded as personalities or sentient beings. Any such address is only by way of apostrophe or ill-temper. Such a scene as that depicted in a recent work on the Kongo, of a native prostrate, praying to his fetish image, is altogether due to imagination and a graphic pen; such a thing we have never heard of, and it is contrary to radical principles.

A fetish, of whatever kind, is but a charm, and imports no more than is conveyed by that word. It is an appeal to the black art for protection and help, as they know nothing of a God who loves and cares for them, and with whom there can be any communication. The gospel of the love of God in its fullest revelation in Christ, brought to bear upon their hearts by the gracious influence of the Holy Spirit, is the only power which can lift these poor people out of their darkness and degradation and satisfy the yearnings of their hearts.

Circumcision is largely practiced in some parts, and is generally performed early, but is by no means universal. It is not a religious rite. The customs of Ndembo and Nkimba are in no way connected with it. It is simply a custom supposed to have some advantages.

There is something which approaches to a sacrifice, although very imperfectly. Blood is some-

A VILLAGE IN THE KONGO COUNTRY.

times used in the weaving of a spell or charm, whether for medicine or any other purpose. The victim slaughtered is called kimenga, and the blood used in the charm or smeared on the nkixi, is called nzabu a menga. Sometimes the blood of a beast slain in the chase is poured out on the grave of a great hunter to insure further success. This ceremony, and libations of palm wine poured out (very rarely) on the graves of great men, are the only traces of ancestral worship, and are not worthy of being thus dignified. The spirit of the dead hunter visiting his grave may be pleased at the sight of the blood, which will recall to him past times. Perhaps it is thought that the spirits of dead chiefs can, in some way, enjoy a libation of the palm wine, to which they were once so addicted.

In concluding this sketch of native customs and superstitions, it may be well to note one or two which help us to express some of our religious ideas. When sleeping in a town on my last journey down from Stanley Pool, I heard at midnight a woman screaming and calling out the name of a fetish, or charm. This lasted for some time, until, not understanding the customs, I felt apprehensive lest some might think that I had bewitched her. I learned, however, that all was right, and in the morning a new phase of fetishism was explained to me. This woman had placed herself under the protection of a charm. She had been to a doctor, who wove mysterious spells, drummed, sang, and danced, gave her something to drink, made certain articles of food taboo, and behaved in such a wild and strange manner that he was able to persuade her that a certain fetish influence or spirit had entered into her, which would bring her luck, would protect her from evil influences, and which, should a witch approach her to do her harm, would arouse her to a sense of her danger. On the night in question the poor woman had a bad dream, and, waking with a sense of horror, believed that her good fetish spirit had made known to her the approach of a witch. So, rushing out in wild excitement, she screamed and shouted to the fetish, and thus tried to frighten the witch.

We can use their phraseology to explain how we may be brought under a higher, holier, and more blessed influence. They can the better understand how our Heavenly Father will give us his Holy Spirit, who will dwell within us to be our guard and guide, to warn us against wrongdoing, to protect us from our spiritual foes, and to purify our hearts. That woman's dream gave us words to express most graphically and intelligibly the great truths of which they in their darkness still had a shadow.

Another custom helps us. When a slave has a bad master, who ill-treats him, and who may, perhaps, intend to sell him on the coast, the slave will run away to a chief who has a good name in the country, and tell him that he has come to be his slave.

If the chief is willing, he orders a goat to be killed; the chief and the slave eat goat together; the covenant is made, and the new slave is called a "goat." His old master hears that his slave is with the other chief, and comes with bluster to demand him back. The new master refuses to give him up in spite of all threats, and finally the old master is obliged to accept a fair price. Slaves thus obtained are much esteemed, for they are generally faithful, and, having thus made their choice, are not likely to run away again. Sometimes free people in trouble will thus become slaves for protection.

So, borrowing their terms, we can urge the dear lads of our schools to take refuge with the Saviour, who will redeem them from a more terrible bondage, and deliver them from the power of the evil one; a Saviour who will be their protector, and who will take them to live with him; a Master in whose service is truest freedom. We have reason to believe that some of our lads have taken the Saviour thus to be their Lord and Master, and, trusting in him for pardon, rejoice to consider themselves his "goats."

Our couriers came in one day and told us that they had seen a man killed on Mbimbi Market. A chief had caught a man for debt on market day; and, as there is a stringent law to provide perfect security on market day, the chiefs sentenced the offender to death. He was allowed to find a substitute, and bought a slave in a neighboring district,

This poor innocent man was beaten to death on the market in the place of the chief. We have thus words and ideas to aid us in telling the story of the loving Saviour, through whose blood we have redemption, pardon, and reconciliation.

Trade and commerce appear only to increase the wickedness and cruelty, for while their influence quickens the intelligence, activity, and industry of the people, it can have no moral and spiritual effect. It is best that there should be both legitimate traders and missionaries, each working in his own sphere. Trade will but seem to elevate to a certain point. The gospel only will work the radical cure.

The children, passing in numbers through our schools, understand many of the evils which degrade and enthrall their fellow-countrymen, and deplore them. When they grow up, they will form a party, which will in time make itself heard; and as the young people have much influence in a town, changes may take place fairly soon. But it all means steady, persistent work.

CHAPTER VIII.

MISSIONS IN CENTRAL AFRICA.

UNTIL the missionary explorations of Dr. Livingstone had given us the knowledge of the interior of Africa, nothing could be done towards the evangelization of its teeming populations; all effort was confined to the coast.* The Church of England Missionary Society were carrying on their work at Mombasa, commenced in 1844 by Dr. Krapf, and after the early decease of Bishop

---

*In a discourse delivered before the American Colonization Society, January 19, 1890, E. W. Blyden, LL.D., made this remarkable statement:—

"In the fifteenth century the Kongo country, of which we now hear so much, was the scene of extensive operations of the Roman Catholic Church. Just a little before the discovery of America thousands of the natives of the Kongo, including the most influential families, were baptized by Catholic missionaries; and the Portuguese, for a hundred years, devoted themselves to the work of African evangelization and exploration. It would appear that they knew just as much of Interior Africa as is known now after the great exploits of Speke and Grant and Livingstone, Baker and Cameron and Stanley. It is said that there is a map in the Vatican, three hundred years old, which gives all the general physical outlines and the river and lake systems of Africa, with more or less accuracy; but the Arab geographers of a century before had described the mountain system, the great lakes, and the source of the Nile. But just about the time that Portugal was on the way to establish a great empire on that continent, based upon the religious system of Rome, America was discovered, and instead of the Kongo, the Amazon became the seat of Portuguese power."

But the work of the Roman Church at that time nor subsequent could hardly be called evangelical.

Mackenzie, of the Universities Mission, Zanzibar became the seat of the bishop of Central Africa.

The whole burden of the work rested on Dr. Livingstone's shoulders. For him the end of the geographical feat was the commencement of missionary enterprise; misunderstood by most people, he endeavored, single-handed, to solve these geographical problems which must be mastered before Christian missions could be commenced on practical and comprehensive lines.

The salient points were ascertained, while his marvelous journeys drew attention to the peoples and their needs. He went to open the door to Central Africa; he flung it open wide, and when the news of the doctor's death reached England, it was felt to be a call to the Christian church for a new and worthier effort for the evangelization of the Dark Continent. From that time commenced that development of missionary enterprise which is now steadily and surely overcoming the difficulties which kept Africa so long secret; and already we are not far from the time when chains of mission stations will cross the continent.

The first to move was the Free Church of Scotland, followed at once by the Established Church

In May, 1875, the first party started to ascend the Zambesi, and by way of the Shire to reach the Lake Nyassa. They took with them in pieces a steam launch, the Ilala; putting her together at the Kongone mouth of the Zambesi, they ascended as far as the Murchison Cataract on the Shire River. There the steamer was again taken to pieces, transported, in seven hundred loads, past the cataracts, reconstructed, and, in October, they steamed into the Lake Nyassa; a week later the foundation of the Livingstonia settlement commenced. There are now several stations on the lake, school work is being energetically carried on, the New Testament has been printed in Chinyanga by Dr. Laws, and everything is full of promise.

The Established Church of Scotland has its mission at Blantyre, near to the Murchison Cataracts; and lately the Universities Mission has undertaken work at Chitesi's, on the eastern shore of the Lake Nyassa; they have also a steamer.

Beside these societies, the African Lakes Company has been formed for commercial purposes, seeking to develop the resources of the country and the industry of the natives, and while carrying on trade on a sound business basis, to do so on Christian principles.

To-day they are prepared to book passengers and goods from England as far as the northern end of Lake Nyassa, from which point the Stevenson Road is in process of construction, to the southern end of Tanganyika. This work has been delayed in consequence of the death of Mr. Stewart, the engineer in charge; and Mr. McEwen, who went to take his place, also succumbed to the climate. It is to be hoped that before long some society will be able to undertake mission work on the headwaters of the Kongo, reaching Lake Bangweolo by way of Lake Nyassa, and so on to the Luapula and the Lualaba.

A letter from Mr. H. M. Stanley, which appeared in the London *Daily Telegraph* of Nov. 15, 1875, giving an account of his visit to Mtesa, the powerful king of Uganda, on the northern shore of Lake Victoria Nyanza, spoke of Mtesa's earnest desire that Christian teachers should be sent to his country. A few days later, an anonymous friend offered $25,000 to the Church of England Missionary Society, towards the establishment of a mission on the Victoria Lake. A similar offer of $25,000 followed a day or two after. The offers were accepted, and in the middle of the following year the pioneer party of the mission reached Zanzibar. A line of stations has now been established between the coast and Rubaga, the capital of Uganda, at Mamboia, Mpwapwa, Uyui, and Msalala. Although the missionaries have experienced much difficulty from the first, and since Mtesa's death a fierce persecution has raged, still the mission has steadily advanced; some eighty natives have been baptized, including one of Mtesa's daughters. Schools and translation work have had a good influence, and the blood of the martyrs at Uganda, as elsewhere, is proving "the seed of the church."

The old mission at Mombasa, Kisultini, and Frere Town, is still being carried on, and is extending its operations into the interior. It is hoped that soon a shorter route to the lake may be opened up from Mombasa by way of Mount Kenia, on the lines of Mr. Thomson's recent journey.

The Universities Mission has its headquarters at Zanzibar, whence its operations are carried on on the mainland opposite, in the district behind Mombasa, and on Lake Nyassa.

The United Methodist Free Church has also a mission in the interior, behind Mombasa.

In 1877 the London Missionary Society, aided by the generous gift of $25,000 by Mr. Robert Arthington, of Leeds, undertook mission work on Lake Tanganyika. They now occupy Urambo, in Unyanyembe, and Uguha, on the western shore of the lake, also Liendwe, at the southwestern end, where they constructed their steamer, the Good Tidings.

The Arabs have so harassed the districts round the lake that mission work is very difficult and trying; but when the steamer is complete, a station will be built at the southeastern corner of the lake, which will be the terminus of the Stevenson Road. In the meanwhile, progress is being made in acquiring the language.

Thus, in spite of toil and difficulty, privations and losses, the continent has been attacked from the east coast, and in less than ten years the best strategic points have been occupied. Neither has there been any crowding of several missions on one spot. The field is large, and each of the great societies is far apart from the other, but so arranged that between them the best points and most practicable lines have been taken.

The same policy was carried out on the southwest coast. The Baptist Missionary Society have been established in the Cameroons district since 1845; and four hundred miles further to the south, the American (North) Presbyterian Church carries on the mission founded in 1842 at the Gaboon. Neither of these missions have been able to make much progress into the interior, and each has been lately brought almost to a standstill by the harsh and arbitrary action of European governments.

Several years ago the French governor of the Gaboon made a law that there should be no instruction in the native language. Everything was to be on the lines of the French normal schools; other harassing restrictions were made, calculated to close the Protestant schools, and the utmost has been done to drive out the American missionaries, and indeed all foreigners, traders, etc., other than French. The schools have been closed, but otherwise the foreigners have not been driven away. All are hoping for a better, more reasonable, policy.

In 1885 the German Government, in quest of unannexed lands on the African coast, took possession of the Cameroons. They treated the Baptist missionaries in a shameful manner; suffice it to say that the policy of the French in the Gaboon has been followed, with greater determination and energy. Feeling that it was impossible to Germanize their new colony so long as the English missionaries were present who had reclaimed it from savagery, they determined to drive them away, and the mission had to be abandoned. This arbitrary action on the part of the civilized governments rendered hopeless any attempt to reach the Kongo Basin from the west coast by any route other than the great river itself, which, happily, has been declared open and unrestricted to missionaries and traders.

Before giving particulars of the two missions on the Kongo, it will be best to note the other missions along the coast. In 1885 Bishop Taylor, of the American Episcopal Methodist Church, started with a party of twenty missionaries, intending to enter the continent by way of Loanda and the Kwanza River, to establish a chain of stations as far as Nyangwe, on the line of Pogge and Wissmann's recent journey. At Nyangwe they hope to meet with a like party starting from the east coast—a grand idea, and by no means impracticable. Many of the missionaries are accompanied by their wives and families, and there is an idea that after a station is built it can become self-supporting. We have reason to fear that the hardships of the pioneer work will lessen this brave band, and prove specially trying to the women and children; but the self-supporting idea could only be entertained by those ignorant of African life and circumstances.* This

---

*Although some of the leading explorers coincide with this opinion of the author, there are evidently good arguments in favor of self-supporting missions. True, some of the missionaries connected with the expedition referred to did

will be a matter of painful experience; but as the mission comes face to face with the difficulties and realities, we may expect that more practical lines will be adopted, and that, with the necessary reinforcements and supports, their grand scheme will be carried out. Such a party as twenty missionaries, with wives and families, must be very unwieldy and difficult to provide for, arriving, as they did, on the coast without any previous experience or friends.

We would not criticise, but only suggest that, in these days, when so much information about Africa may be obtained, it is well for those who contemplate founding new missions to use every precaution to minimize risk and difficulties.

---

suffer great hardship, yet the self-supporting theory cannot, therefore, be set down as a failure. The writer of this note heard Bishop Taylor, in 1890, relate some of his African experiences, and he was then quite sanguine of the success of the plan of self-support,—of course after the stations should be fairly equipped and set to work.

In a fertile, well-watered, well-timbered country, capable of producing almost anything that grows, why should not a mission, after getting a start, support itself? The choicest spots are the most-thickly inhabited, and there is where stations are generally planted. How was it with early missions among the western Indians of America, before the government began to support them? The Shawnee, the Iowa, and the Pottawatomie missions, and various others, were not only self-supporting in a short time, but became wealthy institutions.

Faith in God is the true idea of missions. Not to be a burden upon others is one of the first practical lessons of Christianity. Following that is the idea that "freely ye have received. freely give." Those to whom the message comes should early be taught the duty of burden-bearing, and the privilege of being co-laborers with God. The doctrine that missions are to be carried by some wealthy society will not inculcate the sense of self-denial on the part of converts, especially converts reared amid the innate indolence of savages. It is rather a bid for them to follow the Master for the loaves and fishes. Means raised for missions should be made to reach out to new stations and new fields as far as possible.

At the end of the chapter on "Missions on the Kongo" is a report of Bishop Taylor to the Africa Conference, which incidentally touches upon this subject.

The next point occupied along the coast is Benguela, whence the missionaries of the American Board had extended their operations as far as Bihe (Ovihe). The intrigues of Portuguese traders resulted in their being driven away from Bihe and Bailunda, and nearly all the party returned home. We hope, however, to hear shortly that the work, which commenced with so much promise, has been resumed, and that the southern districts of the Kongo Basin may be evangelized by that agency.

So the various societies are attacking the continent from the west coast at points about four hundred miles apart. Roman Catholic missions have been established in the Gaboon territory, also at Loango, Landana, on the Kongo as far as Stanley Pool, in the Portuguese possessions south of the Kongo, and on the Cunene River.

On the east coast they are at Zanzibar and Bagamoyo; also on the Victoria Nyanza and Tanganyika Lakes, and on the Zambesi River.

CHAPTER IX.

MISSIONS ON THE KONGO RIVER.

NOW as to the Kongo River, and the Protestant missions established there. When the missions had been established on the great lakes, Mr. Arthington, of Leeds, wrote to the committee of the Baptist Missionary Society, offering them $5,000 if they would undertake mission work in the Kongo country, and in districts east of Angola, where there had been Roman Catholic missions in time long past. The society accepted the offer, and sent instructions to two missionaries at the Cameroons to prepare for a preliminary journey in the region to be occupied.

Scarcely had these steps been taken, when the news reached this country of Mr. Stanley's arrival at the mouth of the Kongo, having traced the course of the river from Nyangwe, and thus discovered a water highway into Central Africa. At once the field of the new mission became enlarged almost indefinitely. In January and April, 1878, journeys of exploration were made by Messrs. Grenfell and Comber, and the latter returned to England to confer with the committee and to seek for help in this enterprise. While these preliminary investigations were being made, a party arrived on the river to found the Livingstone (Kongo) Inland Mission (undenominational).

In June, 1879, Mr. Comber returned with three helpers, of whom the writer was one. We made our first station at San Salvador, the old capital of the Kongo country, about seventy miles south of the highest navigable point of the Lower Kongo. The natives of the upper river bring their ivory and produce in canoes to Stanley Pool, and there all has to change hands, as the river is not further navigable. The natives of the cataract region buy at the Pool, and convey to the white men on the coast. One of the great trade routes passes close to San Salvador, and we hoped that these traders might carry our stores and help us to Stanley Pool. They, however, in spite of all we told them of our errand, steadily and persistently refused to allow us to go to the Pool. "No," they said, "you white men stay on the coast; we will bring the produce to you there; but if you go to the Pool, you will know our markets and buy where we do; our trade will be lost; then how shall we obtain our guns and powder, beads and brass, crockeryware and knives, cloth, and all the fine things we get now? No, we will never let you pass our towns; and if you persist, you will be killed." They could not conceive of people who were not traders.

We built a stone house, and prospered nicely in

our work at San Salvador, but beyond the king's territory we were blocked by the native traders. Thirteen attempts were made, first on one road and then on another, until Mr. Comber was attacked and shot. He was able to escape, and the bullet was extracted.

Then followed long palavering, and at last the road was declared open. Meanwhile, we learned that Mr. Stanley had returned to the Kongo, and was engaged in making a road from Vivi, on the north bank of the Kongo, from the point where the river ceased to be navigable. He was said to be acting for the king of Belgium, and to have instructions to open up communications between the coast and Stanley Pool. This was good news indeed. Next we learned that a M. de Brazza, who had for a long time been exploring inland from the Ogowe River, near the equator, had come down onto the Upper Kongo, thence to Stanley Pool, and by the north bank to the coast. As the south-bank road was declared open, it was determined that Messrs. Comber and Hartland should once more try it, while Mr. Crudgington and I should attempt the north bank. The south-bank party met with a repulse in a few days, but on the north bank we were more fortunate.

We found that Mr. Stanley's steamer road extended as far as Isangila, a distance of about fifty miles from Vivi. There we found his advanced party; beyond was unknown land. De Brazza

THE MISSION BOAT, PLYMOUTH.

must have kept some distance from the river, for we, who kept close to the stream, were soon among people who had never seen a white man. There was, however, so little intercommunication between the people that no one knew of Mr. Stanley's approach a day's march beyond his camp. We were, therefore, able to take the people by surprise; and when we reached the districts of the ivory traders, they were bewildered at our sudden, unexpected advent, not having any idea of white men trying to reach the upper river; they had not recovered from their astonishment before we had passed on. So, resting in quiet places, and traveling rapidly in this way, we were able to reach the Pool, and visited Ntamu, where now Léopoldville and our Arthington Station are established. Having accomplished all that we desired, and ascertained the correct geographical position of Stanley Pool, we returned. It was a risky, adventurous, anxious journey, but we accomplished it in safety, and were thus the first who had made the journey from the coast to Stanley Pool.

We found that our brethren of the Livingstone Mission had established their advanced post at Mbemba, on the banks of the Kongo, about eighty miles from Vivi.

Mr. Crudgington then went to England to consult with the committee of the society, and to get a steel sectional boat according to Mr. Stanley's advice. He hoped to be able to navigate a reach of about ninety miles of the cataract region, from Isangila to Manyanga, a distance of only eighty-five miles from Stanley Pool; he advised us to do the same. Mr. Crudgington brought out the boat, the Plymouth, which we transported to Isangila, and then were able to establish ourselves beside the International Association at Manyanga.

After a few months Mr. Stanley kindly offered us a fine site at Stanley Pool, which we gladly accepted and occupied in the autumn of 1882, calling it Arthington Station.

Some months after, the Livingstone Mission arrived, and obtained a site from the International Association. Thus far the two missions are arranged alternately along the line. Each manages its own transport service, which is a severe task on those who have to attend to it—so severe, indeed, that we cannot arrange ourselves so that each might help the other, although we should like to do so; but, as it is, we can find sufficient carriers, and maintain the transport in an effective manner. When the natives saw that we were transporting by water, and thus avoiding their opposition, they opened the roads, and were willing to carry. We therefore, gladly relinquished the cataract water, and now all is conveyed by land from Underhill, our first station on the south bank, nearly opposite Vivi, to Stanley Pool, a distance of about two hundred and twenty-five miles.

Everything is carried on men's heads from station

TRANSPORTING A SECTION OF THE BOAT.

to station. The Baptist Mission has four stations between the coast and Stanley Pool inclusive. The fifth station, San Salvador, is off the line. The Livingstone Mission has six stations up to the Pool. A Portuguese Roman Catholic mission soon followed us to San Salvador, but they have not been able to do much to trouble us.

As soon as the transport service was working properly, Mr. Grenfell, of the Baptist Mission, went to England to superintend the construction of a steamer for the Upper Kongo. It was called the Peace. The whole expense was generously met by Mr. Arthington. The Peace was built by Messrs. Thornycroft & Co., of Chiswick; she ran her trial trip on the Thames. The vessel is built of galvanized steel, is seventy feet in length, and propelled by twin screws. After her trial trip she was taken to pieces, and sent out to the Kongo in that state.

Arrived at Underhill, she was transported over the two hundred and twenty-five miles to the Pool, on men's heads, and everything reached there safely; of the thousand and one parts that go to make up a steamer, nothing was missing. Two engineers were sent out to reconstruct her, but they died of fever before they arrived at the Pool. When the news reached England, another engineer was sent out. He, too, died on the road up.

Mr. Grenfell had then to build the steamer himself, and, having great engineering ability, he was able to instruct his native assistants in the art of riveting. Having placed a part in position, they drove the rivets, and did their work so carefully and skillfully that, when the time came to launch the Peace, she was found to be a perfect success—no leaks—as nicely riveted as if European workmen had put her together.

The Livingstone Mission has also a stern-wheel steamer, the Henry Reed, built by Messrs. Forrest. She, too, was transported in the same manner, and was reconstructed after the Peace was launched, on the same stocks, by Mr. Billington, of that mission.

Mr. Stanley has also three steamers on the Upper Kongo, and a fourth had, by the last mail, nearly reached the Pool. The International Association had by this time acquired sovereign rights over large districts in the cataract region of the Kongo, and in the valley of the Niadi Kwilu. It had also established itself at the equator, beyond which Mr. Stanley had continued the work, over the whole length of the navigable river, to the Stanley Falls, one thousand and sixty miles, exploring several branches, upon which he found two new lakes. Treaties were made with chiefs over the whole length, stations and military posts were placed among friendly people, and a station was established at the Stanley Falls.

While this was going on, various circumstances were bringing Africa very prominently before the eye of Europe. Germany was annexing freely along the coast. Complications arose in consequence of this. There were difficulties in reference to Angra Pequena, the southeast coast, and the Niger; there were troubles between the French Government and the International Association. Portugal proposed to annex the mouth of the Kongo. An annexation fever was in the air. To prevent the breaking out of serious trouble, a conference of the great powers of Europe was called.

It was now time for the International Association to explain its position, and to seek a recognition of its acquired rights.

When the news of Mr. Stanley's great journey "across the Dark Continent" reached Europe, King Leopold, of Belgium, conceived the idea of opening up the vast newly-discovered regions to the benefits of civilization and commerce. It was felt that such a work could not be accomplished unless the whole region could become a free State. It was rightly feared that, as soon as the importance of the basin became known, France or Portugal might annex the mouth of the river, and thus destroy all hope of future development. In their colonies near the mouth of the Kongo, both France and Portugal so hampered trade with heavy duties and restrictions that comparatively little could be done. Then, again, there could be no future for the Free State without a railway to convey the produce from Stanley Pool to the coast. With such a means of transport, the whole country, with its vast resources, would be placed within easy reach of

Europe. Were a single company to attempt this, it would soon be ruined by the greed or false economy of France or Portugal. Quietly, but energetically, therefore, the association acquired sovereign rights, until France and Portugal threatened to annex. When the conference commenced to sit, these two powers each made large demands.

European jealousies, however, prevailed to thwart this greed. The other powers saw no advantage in allowing either France or Portugal to annex, and keep for herself, this newly-found continent; so, first, they agreed that the whole region of the Kongo Basin should be thrown open to the commerce of all nations.

Since Europe had thus declared herself, the district was scarcely worth so much in the eyes of France. Accordingly, she consented to recognize the sovereignty of the association, on condition that large tracts on the right bank of the Kongo were ceded to France. It was an unsatisfactory bargain, but it was either that or nothing for the Free State. Accordingly, the French boundary is extended from the Gaboon down to five degrees south latitude, thence following the line of the Chiloango River to its northernmost source, whence the line strikes the Kongo a little above Manyanga; the river then becomes the boundary until near the equator, after which the eastern watershed of the Likona is the limit.

Portugal was very obstinate, and an identical note

from England, Germany, and France was necessary to bring her to terms. It was finally arranged that the Portuguese boundary should be extended to the south bank of the Kongo as far as Wanga Wanga, a distance of ninety-five miles; then to follow a line, due east, on the latitude of Noki, as far as the Kwangu River, including, also, a small piece of coast line near the French frontier.

The other powers readily recognized the Free State, which had thus a coast line of twenty-three and one-half miles. The conference had, meanwhile, decided that the whole of the Kongo Basin should be thrown open to free trade without any restriction, and added to the region a coast line from Setta Cama to Ambriz. Avoiding the watersheds of the Nile and the Zambesi, it is extended to the Indian Ocean. The north bank of the Zambesi to five miles above the confluence of the Shire is included, also the basin of the Shire, and the Lake Nyassa. Thus both the Scotch missions and the African Lakes Company are safe.

Beside the most rigid injunctions enforcing free trade, absolute religious liberty and freedom of worship are guaranteed; special favor and protection is provided for all missionaries and religious and scientific enterprises. The slave trade, also, is not to be tolerated in any part. King Leopold, of Belgium, will assume the sovereignty of the Free State.

We cannot fail to see the hand of God in this result. Those who have been watching the development of affairs can but wonder at the marvelous providence which has guided all. Now, with such a sovereign, and such a charter of freedom, we can but look forward with the fullest hope to the future of the Free State of the Kongo (*l'Etat Independant du Kongo*).

The Livingstone Mission has, since the first of January, 1886, been transferred to the American Baptist Missionary Union. The best understanding exists between the two societies on the field; there is room for all the energy and force that each can bring. Although on the line of transport we are compelled to keep near to each other, on the great upper river we must keep far distant, if we would wisely and thoroughly occupy this vast field. As to its openness and readiness for missionary effort, let the last news received speak. Mr. Grenfell had recently returned from a voyage in the Peace over the whole length of the river to Stanley Falls, exploring several affluents, a journey of over four thousand miles, one-third of the voyage being in waters never before visited by any European. One of the affluents, the Mobangi, he traced for four hundred miles as far as four and one-half degrees north latitude, and when he turned back, it was still a great river, and navigable probably for a long distance. It is believed to be identical with Schweinfurth's Welle, and if so, we have a highway to the Southern Soudan.

PUTTING SECTIONS OF BOAT TOGETHER.

The Baptist Missionary Society intend, as soon as possible, to place ten stations, say one hundred miles apart, along the one thousand and sixty miles of clear waterway to Stanley Falls, each in the best strategic position, which will be centers for further operations on the great branches of the Kongo and the surrounding districts. Mr. Arthington presented the mission with a further donation of $10,000, on condition that, as soon as practicable, its operations should be extended as far as the Lake Muta Nzige (about two hundred and fifty miles), where we hope, before many years have elapsed, to join hands with our brethren of the Church Missionary Society, working westward from Rubaga in Uganda (distant about two hundred miles), and our brethren of the London Missionary Society, working northwards from Lake Tanganyika (about one hundred miles).

There must be much patient work before that be accomplished; but the time is by no means distant when the workers from the east and those from the west shall join hands in the center of the continent. If so much has been accomplished in ten short years, what may we not look forward to in the future? Our great Master is with us, planning, guiding, strengthening, and sustaining. Cost what it may in life or treasure, we must not abate our efforts until all parts of Africa have heard the gospel of Christ.

In 1890 Bishop Taylor, of the Methodist Episcopal Church, submitted a report of his missionary charge in Africa, of which the following is the part referring to the Kongo District:—

"A march of about one thousand miles from Malange [in the Angola District] brings us to Luluaburg, in the Bashalange country, near the headwaters of the Kasai. William R. Summers, M. D., one of our Angola pioneers, made this march in 1876. On my application the governor-general of the independent State of Kongo gave him permission to found a mission at Luluaburg. He accordingly put up three mission buildings and was proceeding with great zeal in his varied work when, near the end of 1887, he was stricken down by wasting consumption.

"I have conditionally appointed our superintendent at Kimpoko, Bradley L. Burr, and Lyman B. Walker to succeed Dr. Summers, if they can get a passage up the Kasai. We must not only hold that fort, but we must fulfill our promise to the kings and chiefs of the densely-populated regions of the Upper Kasai and Sankuru countries, and plant missions there as fast as the Lord shall lead us.

"From Luluaburg we make a journey of one week on foot to the junction of the Lulua and Luebo Rivers, and thence descend the Kasai by steamer eight hundred miles to its flow into the Kongo, thence down the Kongo seventy-five miles to our station at Kimpoko, on Stanley Pool. James Harrison, M. D., is now in charge at Kimpoko, assisted by Hiram Elkins and Roxy, his wife. In March of last year I received a report from this station [from Bradley L. Burr, then in charge] extending from July, 1887, just before I left, to March, 1889, from which I make the following extract:—

"'An English school (no English children) has been in operation from the first. The station children have attended regularly, but the village children only at rare intervals. Dr. Harrison has charge of the school work. Three of our boys have given up their fetishes and made a profession of having faith in Jesus. They join in all our social meetings, and we believe them to be sincere. With our very imperfect knowledge of the language, Mrs. Elkins, Dr. Harrison, or myself have been quite regular in visiting the villages and in endeavoring to instruct the people.

"'In times of sickness Dr. Harrison has been in the habit of visiting the farther villages, more than a mile distant, twice a day, attending on all who asked for his services. Nearly all the people in this neighborhood have been vaccinated by him, and thus the smallpox, which has been raging in other villages, has been comparatively light here. In regard to every-day station work, Mrs. Elkins has managed the household affairs and assisted in the school work.

"'I have had a general oversight of the station since January 1, 1889. *We have been self-supporting, besides paying out quite a sum for transport.*

[And they have later built a new mission, fifteen by eighty feet.] The plantation, though small, has been a great factor in reducing our living expenses, while the sale of dried meat has kept us in ready money. We have built a house twelve by thirty-six feet for the boys and for a shop, and repaired both the other houses. Though we have had our share of trials and failures, the Lord has given us blessings and victories not a few; so we thank God and take courage.'

"Leaving Kimpoko, we go by boat twenty miles to Leopoldville, at the lower end of the Pool. Then we walked by caravan trail one hundred miles to Manyanga; thence down the rapids in a freight-boat eighty-eight miles, to the lower end of the middle passage of the Lower Kongo at Isangila, where we have a transport mission station, with seven acres of land bought of the Kongo Government. Our missionary there is William Rasmussen, who is preaching in the Kongo language in many of the surrounding villages.

"A walk of fifty-four miles brings us to Vivi, the old capital of the Kongo Government. Being a high and dry plateau, I presumed that we could produce but little, hence bought twelve acres of ground, including our mission buildings. It is, however, proving fruitful, and gives promise of *early and ample self-support*.

"A hundred miles by steamer will bring us to Banana, at the mouth of the Kongo, and two hours by canoe or boat lands us at our mission at Natombi, in sole charge of Miss Kildare, an accomplished Irish lady, who paid her own passage to Kongo for the pleasure she has in giving her efficient labors and her life to help save the perishing people of this great continent.

"The families of the Kongo Liberians which emigrated thence last year were settled by the Kongo Government at Natombi, near our station, and twenty of their children attend Miss Kildare's school. We bought of the natives, and then of the government, ten acres of ground, and built an iron house with wood frame, twenty-four by twenty-two feet. Miss Kildare preaches in the villages in the Kongo language.

"Two days by steamship northwest will bring us to Mayumba, and then eighteen miles by boat up the Laguna will land us at our mission station, called Mamby, in sole charge of Miss Martha E. Kah. We have there, by purchase of the natives, recognized and registered by the French Government, one hundred acres of good land, an old house, and a new house nearly finished. The French Government limits our labors there to what may be done in the French language; hence our work is crippled and not promising, but Miss Kah believes that the Lord wants her to wait and work at Mamby; so we must pray for our dear heroic sister, and let her work out the problem."

CHAPTER X.

LONDA LAND (ULUNDA).

LONDA LAND is a region in the more southern Kongo country, and is inhabited by what are known as the Balonda (Ba-Londa) tribes. These include a great number of smaller tribes.

Rev. J. G. Wood, who has written much concerning the peoples and country of Africa, says there is considerable variety of color among the Balonda tribes. Some are of a pale chocolate hue, while others are as black as the blackest negroes.

The men are of a rather pleasing appearance generally, although not free from the ordinary vices of savage life. They are far less cruel and treacherous than many other natives of the "Dark Continent." The women are also exceedingly lively, and spend much time in social chattering. Both men and women go very sparingly dressed, and quite commonly without any clothing at all. As to the matter of keeping warm, however, very little covering is necessary, as their country extends little if any more than ten degrees from the equator.

It is related that one woman, a chief named

Manenko, carried out the extreme of her country's fashion by appearing before Dr. Livingstone with no covering whatever, excepting a few ornaments around her neck and a complete coloring of bright red ocher. This attire she seemed to regard as the height of dignity.

However, the introduction by traders of European dry goods has, to some extent at least, changed their ideas of dress. But the mania for fancy calicoes is not begotten so much of a desire to be respectably covered as to present a gaudy appearance. A very small quantity of cloth goes a good way in displaying the wealth of the wearer. It may be explained that the wealth of the individual is mainly indicated by the ornaments on the person.

The women, like most savages, will purchase fancy cloths and trinkets at extravagant prices. Half a yard or a yard of calico, for which many times its value has been paid in some kind of trade, will be simply tied around the neck, or in some way fastened upon the body. Such decoration gives the wearer quite an aristocratic air, and she feels as thoroughly dressed as would a European city belle in a silk or satin of the latest style.

Having been reared to go without clothing, even the coolest evenings of their equatorial region do not appear to make them uncomfortable. Their whole bodies are as much accustomed to contact with the weather as are the hands and face of people who are used to clothing. If extra heat be desired at night, it is supplied by keeping up a fire. Even little babies are as much exposed as the older people.

The Balonda mother has a very simple mode of carrying her infant. A belt of plaited bark, some four to six inches in width, is hung over one shoulder and under the other. In this the child is seated, face inward, with its little arms and legs entwining its mother's body. But the women are cunning enough to appeal to the sympathies of traders and missionaries by holding up their naked babies, and making them a pretext for begging pieces of cloth. But when such appeals have gained the desired object, it has often been noticed that the cloth was used as an ornament for the mother rather than as a covering for the child.

The desire for ornamentation is conspicuously shown in the various modes of dressing the hair. The hair of the Balonda, although quite "kinky," grows to a considerable length, and many are the ways in which it is "done up." Sometimes on either side in front it is braided or woven and then fastened into the shape of buffalo horns, the back part hanging in curls. Sometimes all the front hair is braided in one tuft, and twisted and fastened in the shape of a unicorn's horn, the back hair falling in curls. Still others dress the hair into ringlets all over and around the head. But the most striking style is the wheel. The basis of this mode is a hoop, which encircles the head in an upright position, passing under the chin; all the hair is made into a line of small braids over the top of the head from ear to ear; then these are spread out and the ends fastened to the hoop, giving the appearance of the spokes of a wheel. Some think this style is designed to imitate the rays of light which apparently dart out from the sun.

The dress of the men, when they dress at all, has more of what civilized people call modesty than that of the women. Yet it is extremely simple, being a girdle around the waist, to which is suspended a piece of dressed skin in front and behind.

A work entitled "The Uncivilized Races of Men" (J. B. Burr & Company, Hartford) gives many interesting facts about the Balonda people. Speaking of their fondness for ornamentation, the author says: "The Balonda men are as fond of ornaments as their wives, and, as with them, the decorations chiefly belong to the head and feet. In some places they have a fashion of dressing their hair in a conical form, while they commonly show their foppery by braiding the beard in three distinct plaits." Having a considerable quantity of thick, woolly hair, they dress it in various fantastic styles.

It is said that throughout a large part of western Central Africa there is one type of knife, which varies somewhat in different districts, according to the skill of the manufacturers. This knife is very large in the blade, requiring a large sheath, which is often highly ornamented. Every man who can afford it supplies himself with a knife.

Heavy rings of copper and sometimes other metals are much in vogue. The men wear them on their wrists and ankles, and, as stated in regard to the ornaments of the women, the wealth of the individual is indicated by the number and size of his copper rings. A rich Balonda man will have half a dozen or more large rings on his ankles, weighing a pound or more each. The walking gait of such a man is necessarily very awkward, as the feet have to be planted widely apart to keep the great rings from interfering. But, as in our own country, the poor try to mimic the rich, and even this awkward style of walking is imitated by those who have no need to do so on account of the greatness or number of their rings. For instance, a young man who is worth only a couple of rings, weighing but a few ounces, will affect the labored strut, with his feet wide apart, as though he could hardly walk for the weight of his jewelry.

Another ornament much prized is a certain kind of shell, from which flat portions are cut and suspended by a string around the neck. These shells are used as emblems of rank, and Dr. Livingstone tells of having received one from King Shinte as the highest token of friendship in his power to bestow.

The matter of salutations is a remarkable feature

of social life. There are several modes of saluting each other, varying according to the rank of the individuals. If a man of low rank should meet a superior, the former immediately drops on his knees, picks up a little dirt, rubs it on his arms and chest, and then claps his hands until the great man has passed. Even great chiefs go through the motions of rubbing the sand, but only make a pretense of picking it up. When one desires to be exceedingly polite, he carries with him some white ashes or powdered white clay in a piece of skin, and, after kneeling, rubs it on his chest and arms. The white powder is a conspicuous proof that the salutation has been properly performed. He then claps his hands, stoops forward, lays one cheek and then the other on the ground. Sometimes instead of clapping the hands, one will beat his sides with his elbows.

Dr. Livingstone, writing of a trip through the country, says:—

"One could detect, in passing, the variety of character found among the owners of gardens and villages. Some villages were the picture of neatness. We entered others enveloped in a wilderness of weeds so high that when sitting on an oxback in the middle of the village we could only see the tops of the huts. If we entered at midday, the owners would come lazily forth, pipe in hand, and leisurely puff away in dreamy indifference. In some villages weeds were not allowed to grow; cotton, tobacco, and different plants used as relishes are planted round the huts; fowls are kept in cages; and the gardens present the pleasant spectacle of different kinds of grain and pulse at various periods of growth.

"Every village swarms with children, who turn out to see the white man pass, and run along with strange cries and antics, some running up trees to get a good view. All are agile climbers in Londa. At friendly villages they have scampered alongside our party for miles at a time. We usually made a little hedge round our sheds, and crowds of women would come to the entrance of it, with pipes in their mouths and children hung to their sides, and stand there gazing at us for hours. The men, rather than disturb them, would crawl through a hole in the hedge. It was common to hear a man running off say to them, 'I am going to tell my mamma to come and see the white man's oxen.'"

It is charged against some of the Balonda people that they have a very clever but rather mean way of extorting money from travelers. When they ferry a party over the river, they purposely drop some article in the canoe, and watch for someone to pick it up. If anyone does so, he is immediately seized and charged with theft, and the party must pay for his freedom. One of Dr. Livingstone's party once fell a victim to this trick, and had to be redeemed before he was allowed to proceed.

The greater chiefs, however, are said to be above such treatment of travelers, and are disposed to show them marked favor. Dr. Livingstone describes a grand reception tendered to him and his companions by King Shinte. The royal throne was spread under a large banyan tree, and covered with a leopard skin. The king had disfigured himself with a check shirt and a green baize kilt; besides these he wore many brass rings and other native ornaments, and a headdress adorned with a large plume of feathers. Three pages stood near him, and a company of women, headed by his chief wife, sat behind him.

In many other parts of Africa the women would have been excluded altogether from a public ceremony, but in Londa the women take part in such meetings. On this occasion Shinte often turned and spoke to them as if asking their opinion. Chief Manenko's husband, Sambanza, introduced the party in the usual manner by saluting with ashes. After him came representatives of the various tribes, headed by their chiefs in the order of their rank, each of the latter carrying ashes and saluting the king in behalf of their tribes.

After these came the soldiers, who dashed at the white visitor in a savage manner, shaking their spears and swinging their shields in a most threatening way. This is their customary mode of doing honor to a visitor, after which they saluted the king and took their places. Then followed speech making, native music, and other ceremonies.

The food of the Balonda is mostly vegetable, and consists largely of the manioc, or cassava, which grows in great abundance. There are two varieties of manioc, one sweet, and one bitter, or poisonous. The latter is most used, because it is of quicker growth. It is soaked in water several days, when the skin is readily pealed off and the poisonous matter is easily extracted. The half-rotten mass is then dried and pounded into a kind of meal. This is cooked into a mush by boiling in water, and has the appearance of common starch when prepared for use. Although the natives are very fond of this mess, Dr. Livingstone says that "to a European it is simply detestable."

That the Balonda do not eat much flesh meat is not because they do not like it, but because they do not have it. Some of them have cattle, and those who have take great pride in them. They are very fond of flesh, and will even eat mice and other small animals with their manioc porridge. Fowls, eggs, and fish are eagerly devoured when opportunity offers. During an overflow of the river, they fix traps and nets in convenient places to catch the fish as the water recedes. In this they are quite expert and successful.

In some respects they are extremely particular in regard to their eating. They will not partake of food which has been cooked by strangers, but will gratefully accept the uncooked food and go by themselves to cook it. When Dr. Livingstone killed an ox and offered some of the cooked meat to some Balonda lords, they would not eat it, although very hungry for meat. They did, however, accept some raw portions, which they carried away to cook after their own fashion.

One tribe was found which would not eat beef at all, because they said that cattle were like men and ought not to be killed for food. There are some other tribes who will not keep cattle, because they say their enemies would make war upon them in order to get their cattle. But they have no scruples about eating the flesh of oxen if it be given to them.

Like many other African tribes, the Balonda make a peculiar kind of beer, which has more of a stupefying than intoxicating effect, and those who drink it are often seen lying flat on their faces fast asleep. A stronger liquor is a kind of mead, which some of them think is to be a cure-all medicine, notwithstanding its manifest opposite effect. King Shinte recommended it to Dr. Livingstone as being good to drive out fever.

There is a curious custom of leaving a home when either the husband or head wife dies. No matter how much labor may have been bestowed to beautify or fortify the place, the custom in such case is to utterly abandon the place. An occasional visit is made in order to make offerings to the dead. This custom accounts for the great number of deserted houses seen by the traveler in passing through Londa Land.

During a funeral ceremony, a continual deafening clamor is kept up. The popular notion is that the louder the noise the greater the honor bestowed upon the dead. Loud wailing, piercing cries, and the constant beating of drums will be continued without ceasing all night long. Oxen are slaughtered for a feast, if the friends can afford it, and much beer or mead is drunk by the attendants. Funerals are, therefore, very costly affairs, as it is thought to be a point of honor to expend much wealth in honor of deceased friends.

Missionaries find it quite difficult to make much impression upon the minds of the Balonda, because of their varied and peculiar notions. They seem to believe that men live after the death of the body, in some way or other, either in the form of some animal or among the deities which they call Barimo. They will admit that there is a Supreme Being, and some will admit that the Son of God became a man, and some other points which are popularly taught as the Christian religion. Then they will suddenly stop and say that may be all well enough for the white men (who they believe all come up from under the sea), but the black men are altogether different, and do not want to go away to some unknown heaven; they want to stay near their old homes.

Perhaps if they were shown the Bible doctrine that the home of the redeemed will be this earth made new, in which all may have an inheritance through faith in Jesus Christ, it would appear to them more reasonable than the mythical theory of immaterial souls with no tangible resting-place. There is no doubt that the *truth* will yet make some of them free.

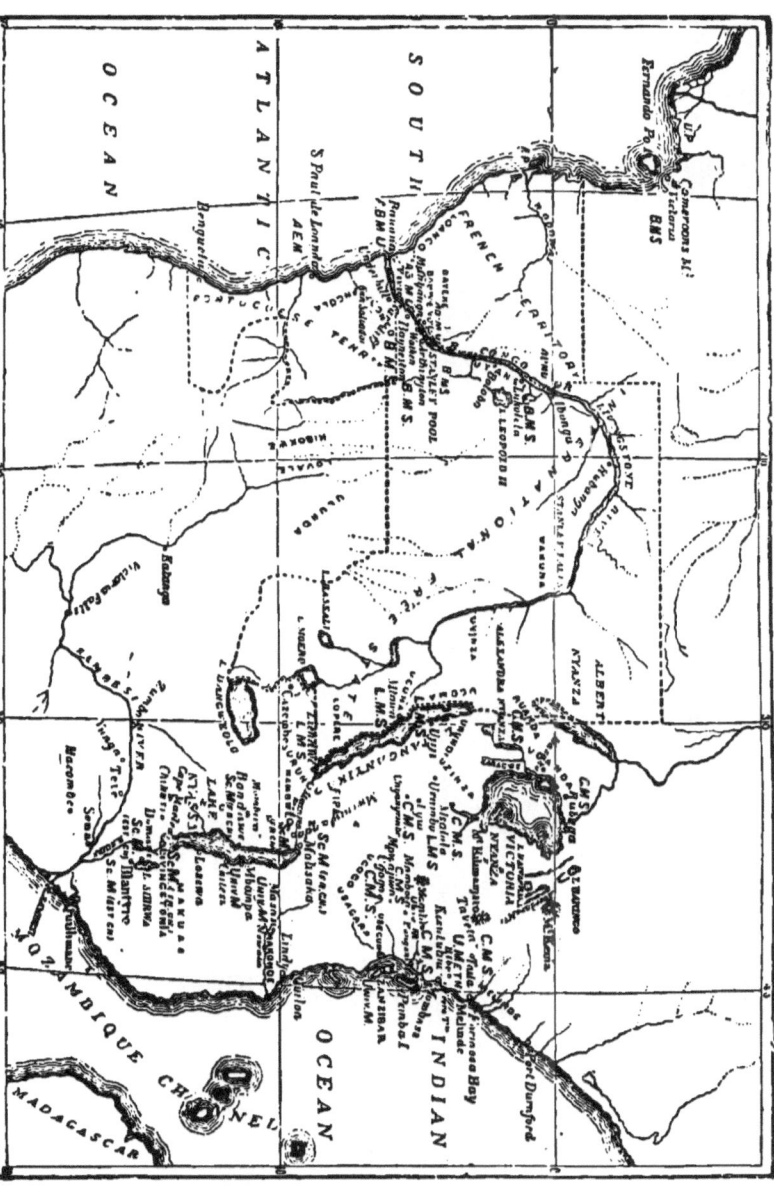

MAP OF MISSIONS IN CENTRAL AFRICA.

C.M.S., (English) Church Missionary Society. L.M.S., London Missionary Society. Univ. M., Universities Mission.
Sc.M., Established Church of Scotland. Sc.M. (Fr.Ch.) Free Church of Scotland. U.Meth., United Methodist Mission.
B.M.S., Baptist Missionary Society. A.B.M.U., American Baptist Missionary Union. U.P., United Presbyterian.
A.P., American Presbyterian Mission. A.E.M., American Episcopal Mission.

CHAPTER XI.

INTERESTING SKETCHES.

REPORT of the American Baptist Missionary Union, in 1889, says:—

"In August, 1886, there was a remarkable movement among the people on the Kongo, who threw away their idols and professed Christ. Great numbers received the gospel at Banza Manteke, and though only two hundred have been baptized, one thousand professed to believe Christ. The readiness of the people at that place and at Lukunga to hear the gospel indicates what we may expect in time to come, judging from their religious condition and the nature of their beliefs. The probability is that they will yield as readily to the pure faith in God and Christ as did the islanders of the sea and the Karens in Burma.

"The great awakening at Banza Manteke in 1866 has been followed by a steady harvest, and a sure increase of the Christians in the grace and knowledge of our Lord Jesus Christ. As the new converts were, of course, almost entirely ignorant of the principles of the Christian religion, and the requirements of a Christian life, the missionaries were cautious not to receive large numbers to baptism at once, but to place them under a course of instruction.

"These converts are very aggressive Christians, and persons have been surprised to come upon people who had heard the gospel where no missionary had been,—to learn that they had been visited by these Banza Manteke Christians. The Upper Kongo offers a promising field in the Bolobo tribes, speaking the common language of the tribes south of the great bend of the river. The steam yacht, Henry Reed, affords means of communication among the stations."

In a recent review of the situation in Africa, the *Baptist Missionary Magazine* gives the following interesting statement:—

"In the Kongo region we find, perhaps, the greatest center of development and promise. The French are acting vigorously in the exploration of the large and attractive territory which has fallen to their share to the north and west of the Kongo; and the French Evangelical Missionary Society, as well as the Roman Catholics, are engaged in the missionary work. The Portuguese seem to be doing little in an official way to open up their territory, but its natural advantages are attracting explorers and traders. The Kongo Free State is by far the most influential factor in the future of the Kongo Valley. The surveys for the railroad from the navigable waters of the lower Kongo to Stanley Pool, at the head of Livingstone Falls, are completed, and a practicable way is found at some distance south of the river, avoiding the numerous ravines which make the present route of travel so difficult.

"There are already ten or eleven steamers on the Upper Kongo, with headquarters at Stanley Pool. Two of these are missionary vessels belonging to the English and American Baptists, who have interesting and successful missions in the valley. One belongs to the French Colonial Government, and the others are about equally divided between the Free State and commercial companies—English, Dutch, and American. Companies have recently been formed for establishing general stores on the Kongo, where everything required for life in Africa may be purchased, and also for conducting a regular transport service between the Lower Kongo and Stanley Pool, pending the construction of the railroad. In the Upper Kongo Valley the natives are realizing the benefits of the improved facilities for commerce, and are bringing the products of that immensely rich territory to the trading stations in increasing quantities. The officers of the State are continuing the exploration of the territory, and every fresh expedition reveals new riches in products and people."

Miss Hamilton, a missionary of one of the northern stations on the Kongo, says in a recent letter:—

"I wish you could see and hear the Christian boys here; they are such fine fellows. They enjoy fun as well as any boys I ever saw, but they are thorough Christians. They go about with us as interpreters when we try to speak to the people, and they enter most heartily into the work, and are always ready with a testimony for the Master. Just now several of them are spending the evening in my rooms, and seem to be very happy. They especially enjoy our photograph albums; and the children here all seem so fond of pictures that I often wish we had a much larger collection for their benefit."

Another missionary relates that "since the death of the old king of Palaba, the people are much more ready to listen and be instructed. They often have nearly a hundred children and young people come together in the little schoolhouse, where the meetings are held, eager to be taught; and even the children are not afraid to pray in public. Their prayers, though short and simple, seem to come from the heart, and are full of praise to God for having sent them the knowledge of Christ. They understand where the money comes from to support the mission, and they do not forget to ask God to bless all those who send it."

A little story, published in the *Missionary Herald*, shows that the old martyr spirit still abides, and sometimes in very youthful bodies:—

"A little slave boy, only twelve years old, surprised the missionaries one day by praying in the boys' meeting. He had not been counted among the converts, and no one seemed to know anything of his previous history. A few days later a feast in honor of some traditional departed spirit was held at his village, and the chief, observing that this boy did not drink beer, commanded him to do so. The resolute little fellow refused, and remained firm, though the chief tried threats and taunts of all sorts. As a last resort the boy was tied and cruelly beaten, and the chief threatened to sell him away from his people to a notoriously hard master. Some of the old men then interfered, and the lad was released, when he came directly to the mission.

"'Did they make you afraid?' asked the missionary.

"'No,' he replied, 'there was no fear in my heart. Jesus gave me strength. They may tie and beat me, or sell me, but they cannot make me drink beer.'"

A Kongo chief, named Essalaka, told the following touching story to an explorer named Captain Coquilhot:—

"You know the big island near my town," he said. "Well, yesterday, soon after the sun came up, one of my women and her little boy started for the island in a canoe. The boy is about twelve years old. He says that while his mother was paddling, she saw something in the water, and leaned over to look at it. Then he saw a crocodile seize his mother and drag her out of the canoe. Then the crocodile and the woman sank out of sight.

"The paddle was lying in the canoe. The boy picked it up to paddle back to the village. Then he thought, 'Oh, if I could only scare the crocodile and get my mother back!' He could tell by the moving waters where the crocodile was. He was swimming just under the surface toward the island. Then the boy followed the crocodile just as fast as he could paddle. Very soon the crocodile reached the island and went to land. He laid the woman's body on the ground. Then he went back to the river and swam away. You know why he did this? —He wanted his mate, and started off to find her.

"Then the little boy paddled fast to where his mother was lying. He jumped out of the boat and ran to her. There was a big wound in her breast. Her eyes were shut. He felt sure that she was dead. He was strong, but he could not lift her. He dragged her body to the canoe. He knew the crocodile might come back any minute and kill him, too. He used all his strength. Little by little he got his mother's body into the canoe. Then he pushed away from the shore and started home.

"We had not seen the boy and his mother at all. Suddenly we heard shouting on the river, and we saw the boy paddling as hard as he could. Every two or three strokes he would look behind him. Then we saw a crocodile swimming fast toward the canoe. If he reached it, you know what he would do? He would upset it with a blow, and both the boy and his mother would be lost. Eight or nine of us jumped into canoes and started for the boy. The crocodile had nearly overtaken the canoe, but we reached it in time. We scared the crocodile away, and brought the canoe to the shore. The boy stepped out on the ground and fell down, he was so frightened and tired. We carried him into one of my huts, and took his mother's body in there too. We thought she was dead.

"But after a little while she opened her eyes. She could whisper only two or three words. She asked for the boy. We laid him beside her on her arm. She stroked him two or three times with her hand. But she was hurt so badly! Then she shut her eyes and did not open them nor speak again. Oh, how the little boy cried! But he saved his mother's body from the crocodile."

Rev. O. Watkins, of Mahamba, South Central Africa, tells this incident of a witch doctor, who came to hear the gospel in 1885:—

"She came to the service, but sat on the floor close to the doors so that she could go away at any moment. During the service someone touched her, and at once she ran away. Next day Daniel and I went to visit a heathen kraal some two miles distant. There was a great feast, and crowds of people had come from all the country round to celebrate the coming of age of the chief's daughter. This female witch doctor had been sent for to perform certain heathen rites and go through her incantations to make the girl lucky and to keep away from her all evil spirits.

"These rites had been performed before our arrival. When we got there, the great heathen dance had just begun. All the women and girls danced first, and afterward the men and youths. I have only to deal with the female dance. They were all in their heathen finery, and each had an assegai and dancing shield. At the head of the dance, and leader of the whole, was the female witch doctor. She gave the step, and led the chant, which they all sang as they danced, recounting the beauty and virtues of the chief's daughter, the glory of her father's house, and the happiness of the man who should lead her to his kraal as his bride.

"The witch doctor was decorated beyond all the rest. Her body was smeared with red clay, and her hair done into long bags which hung all round her head and face. On her arms and legs she had rings of beads and wide rings of brass. In one hand she held a battle-ax and in the other a shield. But what made her so awful in the eyes of the heathen was that around her neck and waist hung all those dread charms used in witchcraft, by which they believed she could discover every secret thing, from a lost child to a murderer.

"As she jumped and leaped and shouted, as she

changed the chant and step of the dance, she seemed like one possessed of devils. As I gazed upon her, I wondered if it was possible to save a woman like her. My heart went up to God that his divine Spirit might draw even her to Christ.

"A few days afterward, when the people came to salute me, I noticed one woman was very much affected when I spoke to her, and then Daniel told me this was the witch doctor, now sitting at the feet of Jesus, clothed, and in her right mind. The divine Spirit had indeed come upon her, and she could not keep away from the services, and she often came privately to Mrs. Daniel to tell of the burden upon her heart.

"She tried to pray, but said when she did so, it seemed as if evil spirits were dragging her away. Often when trying to pray for mercy in the prayer meeting, she would rush away to the solitudes of the mountains, and there wander about like an unquiet spirit. Little by little more light came to her dark mind, and at last she was able to trust in Christ, who saves to the uttermost.

"She was at once transformed, and her life was changed. The red clay of heathenism was washed away, and she dressed as a Christian woman, with her head covered. All her charms and implements of witchcraft she burned with fire; she would not throw them away lest others should find them and thereby work wickedness. Her witchcraft had brought her great gain, but she gave up all for Christ.

"She had been living with a man who was not her husband even by native customs; she at once left him and came to Mahamba with her little boy. She is now very poor, but very happy, and she works in a little plot of ground where her mealies (maize) grow, and so provides for herself and child. At her own special request she was christened 'Mary Magdalene,' and, like that other Mary, she loved much because much had been forgiven.

"Her conversion confounded the heathen people who knew her; in their eyes the success of the gospel was assured; nothing could withstand it. In many a distant heathen kraal to-day the story is being told by heathen lips to wandering heathen ears, and many will come to Mahamba to know if these things are so."

www.ingramcontent.com/pod-product-compliance
Lightning Source LLC
Chambersburg PA
CBHW030319170426
43202CB00009B/1062